My Lovel
Enjoy this book and
my chapter 17.
Love Yvonne
X

Mindfulness
for
Transformation

A Collection of Stories for Compassion, Courage and
Community

Testimonials

"An inspiring and powerful collection of stories documenting the transformative power of mindfulness to change lives."

James R. Doty, M.D., Founder & Director, The Stanford Center for Compassion and Altruism Research and Education (CCARE), New York Times bestselling author of Into the Magic Shop: A Neurosurgeon's Quest to Discover the Mysteries of the Brain and the Secrets of the Heart

"With our busy lives, these short mindful stories are the perfect way to take a moment to find a little spark of inspiration each day and put the lesson into practice."

Carin Winter, CEO Mission Be, Mindful Education

"An essential and inspirational read for both experienced practitioners and all those who have always wanted to try mindfulness. Highly recommended."

Mark Campion, Mindfulness Teacher, Assessor for the Teach Mindfulness Program, 30 years experience of working with people in potentially high stress environments.

First printing, 2020

ShamashAlidina.com
TeachMindfulnessOnline.com

Cover Design: Emily Canino
Editors: Kerry Laundon and Rachael Chilvers

Table of Contents

Part I:
Finding the Courage to Manage Challenging Experiences

Dedication

I'd like to dedicate this book to all those who have suffered due to the pandemic. I hope mindfulness can offer some peace of mind for you.

Acknowledgements

A huge thank you first of all to all the mindfulness teachers who have contributed a chapter to this book – you courageously opened your hearts to us all and I'd like to personally thank you for your courage in doing that. Also, a very big thank you to Kerry, who acted both as an editor and project lead, working hard to turn all the different voices in this book into a coherent and unique publication. And thanks to Rachael for her editorial support. Finally, thanks to Emily for the cover design and Oprah for typesetting and preparing the book to go to press.

Foreword

This is a book in which a range of authors share how mindfulness changed their lives. I too am passionate about mindfulness, and here is the reason why.

As a medical doctor, I was under relentless pressure. In the last two years of my work in accident and emergency, every day triggered the stress response. I thought it was normal and just kept going, as those around me did.

What I realised through my training and then my practice was that stress was a common state of being, experienced by the majority. It seemed to have become the way of the world and I was falling into its clutches.

I was signed off sick for two weeks. Those two weeks became two years, during which time I travelled to India to study Ayurvedic medicine, mindfulness meditation and yoga. I also travelled to the USA to deepen my knowledge about the neuroscience underlying mindfulness meditation and its impact within organisations. Mindfulness was now a core part of my personal and professional life.

As humans we all navigate a whole range of emotions and experiences, many of which can be challenging to say the least. Most of us meet those challenges and struggles with resistance, wanting things to be different. This causes mental, emotional, physical and social stress, which in turn impacts our personal and professional lives. Mindfulness allows us to be with our experience, resting in awareness and seeing it as it is. This in turn allows for a sense of calmness and clarity from which we can make informed choices and wise decisions.

We all have different paths to travel in life. As you read the chapters of this book you will notice how different each person's life experiences have been, but take a closer look and you'll also realise that mindfulness is a universal practice accessible to all. We all have the capacity to be in the rich, felt experience of the here and now.

The contributors to this book remind us that mindfulness practised in the moment can transform the moment, and mindfulness practised moment by moment can transform lives. The book you hold in your hands is testament to this. Shamash and the Teach Mindfulness graduates authentically share their experiences of mindfulness, and in doing so inspire me to continue to dive deeper into my own present-moment experience. May it serve you so as well.

Dr Reena Kotecha, MD

I've developed the 'Mindful Medics: Healthcare Starts with Self Care' programme, a mindfulness and compassion-based emotional intelligence training course for healthcare professionals across the globe. To find out more, please visit my website.

www.drreenakotecha.com

The Story Behind This Book

This book is a community project. All the graduates from our Teach Mindfulness training programme were offered a chance to write a chapter for this book. And what you hold in your hands is a collection of stories from the brave and generous souls who stepped up to that challenge.

This is actually the second book we've produced together. The first book was born spontaneously in response to the sudden lockdown we faced here in Europe and around the world in the face of a global pandemic.

That book, *Mindfulness for Challenging Times: A Collection of Voices for Peace, Self-care and Connection*, was a huge success. We loved working on a project together, and it ended up being the first mindfulness book to specifically help people through the pandemic and its unique difficulties.

This book is a little different. We realised, after publishing the first book, that it was the stories that people had shared in their chapters that were the most inspiring. Stories that shared how people meet their challenges and overcome them.

So, we thought – why not have a whole book sharing how mindfulness has transformed our lives, in the hope that the stories may inspire readers to either give mindfulness a go or (for those familiar with mindfulness) seek to understand more deeply the difference that mindfulness can make to their lives? This book includes a variety of stories of courage, compassion and community, and we are pleased to be able to share these with you.

About the Teach Mindfulness Community

The Teach Mindfulness Community is made up of graduates of Teach Mindfulness, a three-month online certification programme. There are almost 500 graduates so far, who have trained with us over the years. If you'd like to join the community, visit TeachMindfulnessOnline.com
or email info@shamashalidina.com – we'd love to hear from you.

If you would like to follow my work, sign up for regular updates on ShamashAlidina.com for weekly mindfulness tips, tricks and news. You will then also be able to attend talks and workshops not only by myself, but also by many of the teachers in the Teach Mindfulness Community. Feel free to reach out and connect with the authors of each chapter directly, too, where their details are provided.

Introduction:
Finding Meaning through
Mindfulness and the Observer Self

~ Shamash Alidina

Seemingly, I had everything going for me, just as I'd planned. I'd got myself into a good university. I was studying a subject in demand. I was being sponsored by a big multinational. And I was even earning good money during the holidays.

And yet, as I stood there, outside the endless lines of department stores, I felt totally lost inside. People were rushing past me from all directions, and yet I remained motionless. It was like one of those scenes you see in the movies, with a character holding on to their shopping bags while all the other shoppers are whizzing past at lightning speed.

I was standing in the middle of London's iconic Oxford Street – one of the shopping capitals of the world. I was holding two bags full of brand-new clothes I had been excited about buying for months. And yet, although my hands were full, my heart was empty.

I felt like I'd been lied to. Cheated. Not by any one person, but by society as a whole. "Treat yourself – buy something nice for yourself," they say, and I did exactly that. I had a feeling of freedom where I could buy whatever I wished for from a shop, without worrying about the price tag, and yet... the feeling was so fleeting. The pleasure was gone in a matter of minutes.

I felt sad, lonely and confused. All this hard work, studying and working – all in vain. What was the pointing of working so hard, if the result is a feeling that's as fleeting as a cloud passing through the sky?

I didn't know what to do. I made my way home with my head down, lost in an ocean of negative thoughts. In fact, I wasn't even having the thoughts . . . the thoughts were having me.

Some weeks passed by, and I continued going through the motions of attending lectures and studying, as I didn't know what else to do. The emptiness grew. And then, one day, while standing on the platform waiting for a train, I saw a large poster of the ancient Greek philosopher Socrates. "The unexamined life is not worth living," boldly stated the poster. It was a clever advert for a course in philosophy. That sounded like the polar opposite of what I was studying. *This is what I need to do*, I thought. *Study philosophy!*

I didn't write down the phone number but, one weekend, the thought of that poster returned to my mind. I checked the directory, looked up the phone number and signed up to the introductory philosophy course.

The course was in South Kensington, the same area as my university. I showed up to the large, imposing Georgian building. It looked very fancy! As I climbed the stairs, I felt a mixture of fear and excitement. I was trying something completely new.

Would I understand what they were talking about? Would it be full of older people wondering what I was doing there?

I entered a large room that was even grander than anything I'd expected. Beautiful wooden flooring oozing with character, a chandelier in the ceiling, and a magnificent view of the leafy street from the windows. The room was filled with light on that sunny September morning.

At the front was a large blackboard. The teacher sat smiling at the front, but he wasn't really engaging with the group yet. He just sat quite still – far more relaxed than I thought I would be if I was about to teach 50 people.

Finally, the session started. The teacher spoke with confidence, clarity and a sense of peacefulness that I had rarely encountered.

He introduced us to the course and began with a diagram, which I vividly remember to this day – even though this experience happened 22 years ago.

He drew a simple pyramid diagram. He labelled the base 'unconscious', which he associated with deep sleep. Higher up the pyramid, he labelled the next layer 'low levels of consciousness', which he associated with sleeping and dreaming.

Higher up the pyramid he went, and the next layer was labelled as 'everyday consciousness'. He called this our autopilot way of living – half awake and half asleep. (As it happens, a study at Harvard has found that, for the average participant from the thousands they studied, 47 per cent of the time their minds were wandering in everyday life – and the rest of the time their minds were present with what they were doing. So half and half was surprisingly accurate!)

But he wasn't finished. The top of the pyramid was reserved for 'higher levels of consciousness'. He jokingly said that we didn't need to take drugs to get to those levels – exercises from many Eastern philosophies and cultures could help us to access these higher states. And what's the effect of accessing them? You feel more alive. More awake. The world becomes more vibrant and enjoyable.

He explained that the very purpose of life is to be happy and engaged, and that can only happen when we live in the present moment – not when we're lost in ideas about the past and the future.

That was a strange concept for me. I lived for the future. I never took pleasure from just living in the moment – that seemed like a radical idea. But I was now ready for a new way of living, having experienced my recent deep frustration with my life.

The teacher then began guiding us in what I now call the Mindfulness of Senses Exercise.

We were asked to sit comfortably and begin with focusing on our sense of sight. The exercise heightened my sense of vision. Colours started to get more vivid. Then he invited us to turn to our sense of touch. I managed to feel the movement of air touching my skin, which I'd not noticed before in that way. Next up, smell and taste. And finally, sound. Rather than trying to concentrate on the sounds, the teacher invited us to let the sounds come to us. And it worked! I realised that listening took no effort – it happened by itself. Then he told us to listen to the furthest sounds . . . and the silence beyond the sounds.

This is when things got a combination of weird and exciting for me. I could indeed sense a silence! A silence that was kind of like a feeling. A sense that the silence was always there but I'd never noticed it. And other part of me, the logical left-brain part, was saying it was just my imagination.

Finally, the teacher told us to be aware of awareness itself. The quality that enabled us to be aware of our other senses. And to rest in that awareness. He told us how we are the observer of our experiences. We are awareness itself. In that way, we are observers of our experiences, like someone watching a movie is separate from the screen they're watching. I was able to follow his instructions, and I felt very peaceful and at rest as thoughts, feelings and sensations came and went into my awareness, all quite effortlessly.

When we came out of the meditation experience, I felt really excited. Wow – I felt invincible! It meant that no matter what people said to me, no matter how much pain I experienced and no matter what feelings came to visit me, it didn't matter. They are just the content of my awareness. And I am awareness itself.

Suddenly, from living a life where my happiness was to come in the future, I was given the opportunity to live in the moment! To live as awareness itself. I just couldn't wait to try this out in real life.

I began to meditate and read books at great speed. I discovered that there was a whole line of people, from philosophers to religious followers, who had the answers to my questions. Life began to make sense. My life began to fill with meaning and purpose. I knew what I had to do: learn all this as quickly as possible and teach others too.

I began to meditate regularly and I read all the Eastern philosophical books I could get my hands on. I even stopped going to my university lectures. Studying chemical engineering seemed like an utter waste of time. I could be meditating instead, I reasoned.

I studied books like *The Power of Now* by Eckhart Tolle, *Freedom from the Known* by J. Krishnamurti, *I Am That* by Nisargadatta Maharaj, *Be As You Are* by Ramana Maharshi, *Peace is Every Step* by Thich Nhat Hanh and *Man's Search for Meaning* by Viktor Frankl. I was also fascinated by ancient spiritual texts like the Bhagavad Gita and the Upanishads.

By the end of the term I had read dozens of books, attended many retreats and spent hundreds of hours meditating. I had even introduced meditation classes to my fellow university students. However, when it came to exam time, I thought there was a good chance I would fail. I'd not studied properly and skipped too many lectures.

Although it seems silly for me to have stopped studying, I finally felt free. All my life, I feared failure. What would people think if I failed? That would make me a failure, I figured. But now, I was awareness – part of something much bigger than my individual ego. Whether I passed or failed wasn't the end of the world. Something would happen. I had a greater trust in the universe.

As it happened, I just about passed. After completing my engineering degree, I immediately signed up to train to be a schoolteacher. I wanted to share meditation with kids. It was tough, but teaching was where I found my calling.

I spent ten years teaching in a school where all the children did meditation. I spent the next ten years teaching mindfulness to adults and training mindfulness teachers all over the world.

To this day, I continue to teach what I learnt about awareness over 20 years ago in that philosophy class. We all have a part of us that is beyond our thoughts and feelings, that lights up all our experiences. That magic force is completely unexplained by science. I consider our true nature, as awareness, to be pure, perfect and complete. Everyone has it, and everyone has had a glimpse of it. And the great thing is, the latest research on mindfulness shows that this quality is key to our wellbeing – often called our 'transcendent self', 'meta-awareness', 'observer self' or 'perspective taking'. Science seems to agree – stepping back from your thoughts and feelings, seeing from a larger perspective, is beneficial physically, mentally, emotionally and creatively, and probably spiritually too.

I like to think of it this way: you are not just a wave in the ocean, but the ocean in a wave.

*

If you enjoyed reading my story, you're in for a treat. This book is filled with a wide variety of stories from people from all walks of life who discovered mindfulness in their own unique ways. Their stories may inspire you, or remind you of the value of mindfulness practice and the variety of ways in which such a practice can be helpful.

Some of the authors have gone through tremendous challenges in their lives. They bravely and openly share their difficulties and how mindfulness saved them, in the hope that you too may turn to mindfulness or similar approaches to help you navigate life's many curve balls.

I invite you to take your time as you read the stories. Take a moment to step into each writer's shoes and see the world from their perspective. Just that very process can help grow your empathy and emotional intelligence. And any mindful practices you're inspired to try will only help to improve your wellbeing and resilience.

Mindfulness of Senses Exercise

This is the meditation I described in my story of mindful transformation. It is a great meditation for both beginners and those with more experience.

1. Sit comfortably.

2. Go through each of your senses, for about one minute at a time. Begin with what you can see. What colours do you notice? Be aware of the sense of distance between you and the objects. Notice the shades and colours of what you see. Bring a sense of curiosity to your experience. Now, close your eyes and be aware of your sense of touch. Be aware of the contact of your body on whatever you're sitting on. Next up is taste. Can you taste anything in your mouth? What about smell? What is the scent in the room you are sitting in? Now become aware of sounds both near and far. Let the sounds come to you rather than trying to grasp or concentrate on them. Let the sounds enter into your awareness.

3. Now, take a minute to appreciate the silence between sounds, or a sense of silence underneath the sounds if you can. All sounds arise out of the underlying silence.

4. Be aware of any thoughts that are popping into your mind and the feelings arising and passing. Watch them come and go like clouds come and go in the sky: the way a cloud doesn't stick to the sky, it flows through. In the same way, watch your thoughts and feelings flowing through the sky of your awareness.

5. Rest in awareness as the container of all your experiences. The awareness that lights up your thoughts, feelings and bodily sensations . . . that illuminates all your experiences.

6. Be the observer, the witness of all your experiences. Rest as awareness itself. Nothing to do, nowhere to go. Just being as you are. As awareness itself.

If you found this exercise useful or interesting in some way, then I urge you to practise it regularly – perhaps once or twice a day. I recommend that you try and turn it into a habit and find a certain slot in your routine in which to do this exercise. In a few weeks' time, you may find some pleasant and perhaps unexpected benefits from doing the exercise regularly. If you do, feel free to get in touch and let me know – I'd love to hear from you.

You can access the audio for this exercise at TeachMindfulnessOnline.com/transform.

How to Use This Book

You can read this book in any order you wish. We've designed the order of the chapters so they make sense sequentially, but if you feel drawn to jump from one part of the book to another, that works perfectly well too. Each chapter is self-contained and makes sense on its own.

Each chapter includes a mindful exercise for you to try. The chapters also include a link to a guided mindfulness meditation audio track by the author of the chapter for you to try at your leisure. It can be fun to try the meditation there and then, to connect with the voice of the chapter you have just read. But if you can't listen then, you can just listen whenever the time is right for you. I would recommend you make a note of the meditations you like, and those you want to try in the future.

If you're new to mindfulness, consider getting into a routine of daily mindfulness meditation. This can have many beneficial effects for your mind and body.

I recommend you start with something very small. You can start with just one breath. Or just a few breaths. Find a time in your daily routine to practise your daily meditation. Finding that daily slot is often the key to creating a mindfulness habit.

Good habits form when you feel good about your success – not when you feel bad for not doing the exercise. Once you establish a daily routine, only practise more if you feel like it, because it's easier to stick to a daily habit if you experience some success along the way. Over time you can increase the length of the meditation, but there's no need to rush into longer meditation practices. Slow and steady wins the race.

To freely access all the guided mindfulness audio tracks that go with this, go to TeachMindfulnessOnline.com/transform. You can find a full list of the audio tracks in the Appendix.

Remember, this book is not a replacement for medical advice. If you're feeling overwhelmed, please seek out professional help. If you don't know who to talk to, visit www.befrienders.org, or call the Befrienders or Samaritans in your country. They can provide confidential emotional support, no matter what the cause of suffering.

About Shamash Alidina

Shamash is the author of seven books including *Mindfulness For Dummies* and *The Mindful Way Through Stress*. He offers Mindfulness Teacher Training and Acceptance and Commitment Training, both fully online. He's currently passionate about growing his community in the new Daily Mindfulness Club. He's based in London, UK.

ShamashAlidina.com

Part I:

Finding the Courage to Manage Challenging Experiences

1

Finding Peace and Mutual Acceptance in the Present Moment

~ *Nicky Minter*

It was the 14th May 2011. I was out walking our two dogs when my father rang.

"Nicola, darling, your mother has had a stroke; she's been taken to Salisbury hospital."

BOOM! I will never forget that fateful moment. Those words and the effects of this traumatic event changed our lives for eight years.

Until that phone call, my life had followed a fairly stable course. My husband and I had the usual ups and downs of juggling our work with two children, running a household and a social life. I worked as a therapist in the world of health and wellbeing, so I had several techniques under my belt and a positive view on life, which had helped me through any emotional issues. But then . . .

BAM! The shock and trauma that followed my dad's phone call was incomparable to anything I could have ever imagined. The first month of Mum's time in the stroke unit was a blur of waiting, confusion, helplessness and disbelief. Was she ever going to recover from this? I was constantly worried about her wellbeing and what our lives would look like from then on. My mind raced as I coped with the physicality of travelling 80 miles a day to the hospital, and the emotional stress of supporting Mum and helping Dad. I had moved into 'coping' mode, but I couldn't control my thoughts and feelings or the reactions they triggered, which manifested as shortness of breath, near-panic attacks and exhaustion. My father and I were teetering on the edge of a precipice with no rope and, as far as we could see, little hope.

Not long after this traumatic event, I picked up a book called *The Power of Now* by Eckhart Tolle, which was deeply enlightening and acutely relevant. I was already familiar with spiritual meditation, but I was curious to see whether mindfulness would help me during this time. I attended a mindfulness-based stress reduction (MBSR)/mindfulness-based cognitive therapy (MBCT) course and further teacher training with the Mindfulness in Schools Project (MiSP) and with Shamash Alidina.

I wouldn't have coped in the following months and years while Mum was alive if I hadn't had these resources. These approaches saved me from a potential breakdown or depression – and stopped me from disappearing to a desert island! They enabled me to remain as present as possible to my mother's situation, as well as my own. Despite momentous challenges along the way, I was able to support her in her torment, and the more I continued with the mindfulness practice, the more accepting and patient I became.

After the stroke, my loving, kind, insightful and active 75-year-old mother became wheelchair-bound and desperate. She relied on others for everything at home. She lost her ability to speak audibly and had a reduced level of cognition and short-term memory. Her previous tendency towards over-anxiety increased exponentially. She had been a regular meditator and worked as a spiritual healer at the Bristol Cancer Centre, but she became incapable of using her resources to help herself, and her mental health became almost impossible to treat in these new circumstances. It was devastating for her. She was depressed, demanding and anxious about everything. In short, none of us knew how to cope with her situation.

Mum and I struggled to maintain harmony, but thankfully we had a deep love for one another. We were on a mutual journey with many mixed emotions, one where we both felt trapped. She had so many physical restrictions to overcome – some days she was very sensitive, and others she was feisty and determined.

I began to realise that the calmer and less reactive I was, the calmer and less reactive she was. Early on, I had fallen into the trap of thinking about the future and worrying endlessly about how long we would have to cope with these difficulties, but mindfulness helped me to become aware of my thoughts and return to the present moment. In turn, this helped me appreciate the smaller details, like the times we laughed about light-hearted things, the kindness of Mum's carers, and our shared love of *Strictly Come Dancing*!

Tragically, in 2014, my father was diagnosed with cancer and, after several intense years of helping to care for Mum, he passed away. This added another layer of emotional complexity and stress for our family. After Dad died, Mum moved into a local nursing home. Between visits, her way of coping was to talk to me on the telephone – if she had been able to have an open line to me all day she would have! She needed to inform me of every detail of her troubles, but sadly I couldn't alleviate her torment. If I could have waved a magic wand I would have, but she was unable to accept her situation, at least not until the very end of her life. My brother, who lives abroad, brightened her life by talking to her most days and visited when he could. My husband and children were a tremendous support, along with other close family members, her devoted friends, and a dedicated therapeutic support team. However, her demands on me were relentless.

The benefits of mindfulness in coping with this were invaluable. I began to allow and accept my thoughts and feelings without so much resistance. Whatever arose, I noticed and felt kindness towards it, which helped me to feel calmer, to breathe and to be still with the present moment. This awareness was completely life-changing and transformative. It was such a relief – I realised that perhaps I *could* cope with this situation after all! After particularly stressful afternoons with Mum, I would leave the nursing home, allow my emotions to arise, take some deep breaths and look at the sky, the clouds, the trees. I learnt that I didn't need to trawl over how negative she had been, what had happened or been said, or how I had reacted. I discovered the ability to connect to deeper layers of presence, tolerance and compassion.

I could sometimes be drawn into the story of how difficult things were. I felt frustration because I couldn't change things for her – I needed to scream and shout to release the pressure, and I kept thinking, "Why is this happening to us?" But as time went on, I experienced that the way to process and help her calmly was to go with the flow and keep returning to the healing stillness of the present moment. This philosophy helped me enormously, and I subtly used it with Mum too, depending on her mood! In her moments of calm, she valued and appreciated all my efforts to help her, which was heartening.

In January 2019, I knew our journey was coming to an end. In the last couple of weeks we had both entered a space of tolerance and acceptance – kindness, compassion and peace for our situations and each other. We were aware that this trauma was a gift for us to face our deepest challenging emotions. She let go of the resistance and struggle, and I let go of any attachment to my ego, my future, or my desires to be or do something else other than be here right now. We surrendered. Mindfulness made a difference to both of our lives; for Mum, it helped her to finally be at peace with her struggle. For me, it enabled me to cope, to find solace in the present moment and to accept a situation I had not expected.

I am immensely thankful to have these invaluable and transformative mindfulness tools for life, and I hope that you feel inspired to explore mindfulness further for your own support and wellbeing. For changes to occur, the brain needs repetition and continued practice: positive changes can become habitual and a part of your way of life, so, if it is appropriate for you, try making mindfulness a part of your regular routine as well as using it when needed. It is well worth it!

Mindful Exercise:
Kindness and Acceptance in the Present Moment

This exercise can help you feel grounded and calm when you notice that you are becoming overwhelmed by challenging circumstances. It enables you to bring your awareness into the present moment and feel kindness towards yourself and your thoughts and feelings. You can do this while sitting or lying down.

1. Stop what you are doing and take a few long breaths, feeling your chest rise and fall as you breathe in and out.

2. Notice what you can see, then close your eyes and notice what you can hear. Now feel the sensations against your body of whatever is supporting you. Breathe.

3. Take your awareness down to your feet, like putting down an anchor in a stormy sea, and take a few breaths with your attention on your feet.

4. Pay attention to whatever difficult feelings arise – notice them and take some long breaths, being open and curious. Breathe. If you resist your feelings, that's fine; keep bringing your awareness back to your breath and to your feet.

5. Take your awareness to your heart: feel kindness, like a warm flame, growing and spreading from your heart and throughout your whole body. Breathe and smile.

When you feel ready, open your eyes and pay attention to what is around you. Take the next steps into your day, maybe feeling more peaceful and accepting of any difficulties, or clearer about what can or can't be changed.

Guided Meditation: Peace and Kindness Meditation

This guided meditation helps you to bring your awareness to the present moment and gives you the opportunity to acknowledge your difficult feelings. It also helps you to cultivate peace and kindness towards yourself and any difficult situation. You can listen to the meditation while sitting or lying down. Access the meditation at TeachMindfulnessOnline.com/transform.

About Nicky Minter

Nicky is an emotional wellbeing practitioner, assisting adults and teenagers to release and process past traumas and stressful emotions. Her desire is to help people to feel more resilient, calm and content. Nicky lives near Bath with her family, and she loves nature, music and sustainable living.

https://www.yes-wellbeing.co.uk

2

Transcending Chronic Depression

~ *Fennel Waters*

When I was 17 years old, I met my husband. He was a beautiful, vintage hippy (30 years my senior), very much into self-awareness, taking responsibility for yourself, love, and living life through travel, knowledge and following your truth.

He guided me to look deep into who I was (and who I wanted to be), and he was gentle and firm as I went through the (often messy) process of personal growth – of shedding the many hooks with which society snares our authentic selves. I was also introduced to Wicca and shamanism, and I aligned myself with nature philosophies and practices.

I grew, and it was a fun, loving, difficult, painful, happy and rewarding time in my life. We were together for 18 years before he departed this world in 2009.

I couldn't say that I was unhappy with my life afterwards and, due to the self-development work I'd invested in over the years, I felt

I had a reasonable grip on things for a while. However, I was still going through a truly traumatic experience, and I found myself falling into a deep, dark pit.

As I grappled with my grief, there were plenty of dark periods, frustrations, angry moments, confused feelings, and listless wanderings and wonderings.

I decided to try mindfulness again. When I'd first encountered mindfulness, I'd tried it on my own rather than with a group. But I'd been scared to explore the experience further – I could see it beginning to crack open the unacknowledged feelings I had been avoiding.

Remembering how the start of that powerful expansion of my mind had felt made me decide to return to mindfulness. I completed two courses within 10 months – beginning with mindfulness-based cognitive therapy (MBCT), followed by mindfulness-based stress reduction (MBSR) – giving myself time to digest what I was learning and build a regular practice.

I was astounded by the speed of the results; I felt differently within a few days of starting the first course, which not only brought its own joy, but really motivated me to continue (even though I kept falling asleep during the body scan!).

After three weeks of the MBCT course, I experienced a massive mind shift. I came to some clear insights about my behaviours and reactions. And, because I had chosen to change and was already viewing my experience from an observer's perspective, I was able to really look myself in the eye this time.

These wonderful fresh perspectives allowed me to uncover and work with many challenges on deeper levels than ever before. The main challenge I encountered was this sense of diminished self-worth (and the judgement, guilt and shame that came attached to that). A big realisation was that my husband had valued and cherished me more than I did myself. Surprisingly, I also discovered that I'd been dealing with chronic depression for over a decade.

Discovering the depression was a relief because it helped me put a name to what I was going through, but working with it was really tough: I would sit for days in a funk, crying and not feeling able to face the world or myself.

But I continued my mindfulness practice and, at some point, I noticed that the dark days didn't last as long, and eventually weren't as intense. Other people started to notice that I was more social, more focused and happier in general. All this encouraged me with my practice and motivated me to ask for help with my depression.

I started to see a counsellor, which, in conjunction with mindfulness, brought up a lot of heartache around my lack of self-worth. I had body dysmorphia, and I constantly compared myself to others (often with the rose-tinted outlook that their life was great and I was the only one struggling).

Thankfully, by this time, I had a regular mindfulness practice going, and so I was able to take a more observational view of these thoughts and feelings. I still got upset, and it was a difficult process; however, meditation gave me stillness, insight and support throughout. I started to love myself, and to be grateful for what I had.

Eventually, my mindfulness practice allowed me to release the judgement and to regard my thoughts and feelings with a wonder and curiosity that I hadn't felt since early childhood. I suddenly understood how much pressure I was putting on myself, which was grossly distorted and impacted by a variety of factors – societal conditioning, peer pressure, marketing and lack of education, to name a few.

I also started to not take things personally. I became aware that people are usually wrapped up in their own heads, and that their behaviour towards me was little to do with me, but more about what was going on with them at the time. It was a complete game changer to realise and understand this.

Even when Covid-19 hit, mindfulness helped. I found myself with a whole new box of unknowns, fears, anxieties and worries on a level that I hadn't felt for years. So, I went back to basics and meditated.

After a week of sitting crying, scared journalling, breathing, and allowing myself to do and be whatever was needed (exercise; stay in bed the whole day; read; watch rubbish on the TV; eat well; binge on sugar and fat; get completely drunk one night), I popped out on the other side.

I listened to what the thoughts and emotions had come to tell me (fear and control worries about the future, my health, my finances, and so on) and I accepted the new unknowns, but also – joyfully – I was able to accept and anticipate the start of a new adventure and a societal shift. The world was never going to be the same, but I was able to make peace more than ever before with what was, even if I didn't know what was coming. I felt as if I was going to be okay. This allowed me to thrive during lockdown, and to be in a more connected place than ever with myself.

Today I do my best to live mindfully every day, so much that it has become an unconscious way of living. I am happy and grateful, and I continually feel more and more alive.

Facing my fears was less scary than I imagined, and knowing more about myself has given me so much more power to decide how I want to live. Now, amongst other skills, I am an accredited mindfulness teacher (MBSR), a qualified life coach and a sensual embodiment guide. I enjoy and am passionate about my work, and I adore the life I have been blessed with – every day, no matter what life brings my way.

Mindful Exercise:
Stop/Reflect/Release

This exercise may be helpful when you feel you are losing your way or struggling with your emotions. The aim is to get into the habit of just stopping, rather than becoming wrapped up in your thoughts, feelings and sensations.

You may find it helpful to write the following exercise out and place it somewhere you can easily see it.

1. Whatever you're feeling – hopeless, sad, judging yourself, isolated or alone – **STOP.** Breathe. Focus on all the sensations you experience during five in-breaths and five out-breaths – the cool air coming in; the warm air coming out. Where do you feel the air most (your nostrils, throat, chest, belly)? With each breath, just for a moment, try to allow yourself to stop thinking, stressing or worrying.

2. Calmly come back to how you were feeling. Remember, this is a process – feelings and sensations are not you, just messages for you. Be kind to yourself.

3. **REFLECT.** Where in your body did your feelings materialise? How? Was it a heaviness in your chest? A tightness around your forehead? A sick feeling in your stomach? An ache in your eyes – maybe you felt ready to cry? See if you can look at your feelings from the outside, like looking at yourself through a window.

4. What do you think these messengers are trying to tell you? Are you giving yourself what you need? Do you need a pause? Are you feeling overwhelmed? Do you need to ask for more time, or set a boundary? Do you need to cry and

let go? For another five breaths, allow yourself to feel the messages that have been sent to help you grow. After feeling and hearing their communication, thank them. **RELEASE.**

5. Give yourself a hug, and say thank you for listening to yourself. Take a few moments to reflect and write down any thoughts or feelings that arise.

I hope this exercise helps you to feel able to look at your experiences more objectively, so you can move forward.

Guided Meditation: Finding Your Way Back to Yourself

This guided meditation is influenced by Sarah Blondin and her Live Awake project. Sarah is a beautiful soul who has helped me greatly as I've struggled with the challenges and obstacles of chronic depression. You can listen to the meditation at TeachMindfulnessOnline.com/transform.

About Fennel Waters

Fennel guides individuals, groups and organisations in the UK and France to rediscover their own power. She hosts workshops on a variety of topics, including mindfulness, stress management, decluttering, pleasure and sensuality, and shamanism. You can reach Fennel at fennelwaters@gmail.com.

3

Making
Friends with Anxiety

~ *Robyn Zagoren*

A friend and I were laughing about a shared experience as the waiter placed my lunch before me, a delicious Caesar salad with the works. However, a few bites in, I noticed a disturbing feeling.

My fingers started tingling. The sensation crept up my hands. It moved into my feet, then my legs. Suddenly, my breathing quickened. The muscles in my hands and legs started to cramp. My vision became blurry, my heart began to race and my face felt numb. I was shaking uncontrollably, and my fight-or-flight response set in. Should I get up and run? And if so, where to? I didn't understand what was happening to me. The thought that I would die in a health food restaurant petrified me – the irony! As the terror took over, I couldn't help but laugh as I tried to maintain my sense of humour amidst the angst. Then these physical sensations intensified into a feeling of dread. Everything went black.

It turns out that I was having the first of many panic attacks. The panic would roll over me for no apparent reason, anytime and anywhere. The fear was palpable. I didn't share what was going on with my friends; I was ashamed, thinking that they wouldn't want to hang out with someone who was losing it. I became well-versed at making excuses to avoid situations that might trigger an attack, so I missed out on opportunities. My life started getting smaller. I was 19 years old: the prospect of living my life this way was terrifying and isolating.

My doctors prescribed several different medications to bring me back to a 'normal' state and reduce the number of anxiety attacks I was having per day – sometimes as many as six. They took tests to see if an underlying medical condition was causing the attacks. They had no idea what was wrong with me. One doctor told me I had type 2 diabetes, while another said I was severely allergic to certain foods and handed me an epinephrine pen. Another suggested that my childhood trauma – growing up watching my parents' loveless marriage – was the root cause, and I should join a therapy group. After losing weight (from changing my diet to avoid allergens), they decided I had an eating disorder. The fear of anxiety was making me clinically sick. How did I go from being a healthy college student and athlete to suffering from panic attacks and other medical conditions in a few weeks? It turns out that trauma and stress can play havoc with your health.

A few months into my battle with anxiety (it felt like a war every day), one of my professors asked me to help teach elementary school-age students how to handle stress. A study at Harvard University was evaluating progressive relaxation meditations, using mindfulness. I jumped at the chance; I loved teaching, and I wondered if it might help me, too.

The students would lie on a mat, listening to a recording taking them through contracting and relaxing different muscles in sequence from their feet to their heads. The meditation left them in a relaxed state. Their minds began to recognise when their bodies grew tense, so they could head off the stress response: the fight-or-flight feeling. It was magical. The students loved it. That night I lay in my dorm room and I practised the meditation. Best. Sleep. Ever.

That was my introduction to mindfulness meditation. I started to realise that fear was not infinite, but a guest in my life. How I treated that guest was up to me. I immersed myself in the world of mindfulness.

Each day I practised breathing meditations and body scans. No longer did I wrestle with the anxiety; instead, I opened up to the sensations with full acceptance, compassion and kindness. It wasn't easy. Some days the panic would set in, and it would take everything I had to sit still with those uncomfortable feelings; embrace, accept and learn from them. Eventually, I was able to recognise that the feelings of anxiety didn't last. I began to understand what was happening, knowing that I wouldn't die, no matter how much the panic took over. No longer did I judge myself for being weak, crazy, or any of the other negative labels that would trigger an attack. The negative mind chatter dissipated.

Being curious and accepting were two valuable attitudes I cultivated. I welcomed what I was feeling, why I was feeling this way, and where these feelings had come from. As hard as it was to sit with those difficult thoughts, feelings and sensations, it was also empowering to open up to them and allow them to visit, knowing they wouldn't stay for long.

The difficulties were hard to face, but I felt the most growth and change when I was able to sit with them. I realised that the negative thoughts I was dealing with were learned responses, created through trauma in my childhood and culminating as anxiety attacks. In my family, you never knew what the climate at home would be: screaming, fighting, even a few loving moments or an unnatural silence. For years, my parents wouldn't talk directly to each other; they used me as a conduit for their communication. The emotional eggshells lined the floors, creating a foundation for anxiety.

The more I practised meditation, the more accepting I became. Through mindfulness, I could separate other people's issues (mostly my parents') from mine, and realise that they were 'not my circus, not my monkeys'. The stress melted away, taking with it the panic attacks. Through mindfulness, I could sit back and view my life as if it was a movie. I was able to send compassion to myself as a child and to my parents.

From then on, I related to my parents differently, understood them and forgave them. They did love me and, although it was far from perfect, they had tried their best. My parents no longer had power over me, using me like a puppet to bolster their needs. The strings released, one by one.

As I developed my practice, there were days when the meditations were fluid and days when my mind wandered. The practice was the most important part: I let go of the immediate outcomes and just allowed my experience to be whatever was happening in that moment. I created a space at home where I could go to sit quietly. I found a beautiful tree I could sit under when I wanted to connect with nature as I took deep breaths and let go. I slowed down, stepping out of my manic autopilot life with all the stressors and the expectations that others put on me. I discovered myself.

Working with my physicians, I eventually weaned myself off all medications. I didn't have any of the conditions they had diagnosed. The panic attacks continued to fade over time, and they no longer feel threatening.

Befriending my panic attacks through mindfulness saved me from a life of misdiagnoses and unnecessary medications, and anxiety and I are friends now. I value my panic attacks as a reminder that I need to slow down, take care of myself, and reconnect. I am grateful for the lessons I have learnt through mindful meditation. I have discovered how to move past the fear and embrace life. I am thankful for the gift of acceptance, knowing that I have the resilience to keep moving forward and that my breath is always with me when I need it.

If you ever feel anxious, you may find it helpful to consider the first thing you reach for or try to do to escape it. Instead, try to look at your anxiety differently. Bring in a sense of non-judgement: everyone struggles in different ways, so be patient and kind to yourself.

It's not a straight road, but a wonderful journey you are on.

Mindful Exercise:
Three Claps, Five Senses

When you start to feel anxious, take a moment to calm your mind and focus on your surroundings rather than your thoughts. This exercise will help you soothe your anxiety by connecting you to your surroundings through your five senses: sight, touch, sound, smell and taste.

1. Clap your hands as hard as you can three times. Notice the sensations in your hands and fingers: any tingling, stinging or numbness. Do your right and left hand feel different from each other? Slowly breathe in and out (preferably through your nose) for one minute as you focus on the sensations you feel in your hands. If you can, make the exhale slightly longer than the inhale.

2. Move your attention to notice five things that you can see. Try to pick something you might not usually notice. It can be a colour, an object, the way the light looks on a surface – look for something subtle or a part of something, not the whole.

3. Next, notice four things you can feel. Bring awareness to the texture of your clothes, the contact of your feet with the ground, how your hands feel now, or the temperature of the air.

4. Now, notice three things you can hear. Take a moment to listen to the sound of a fan, a bird, traffic, laughter or perhaps the quiet around you.

5. Next, notice two things you can smell. Bring your awareness to the scent, such as food cooking, lavender, chocolate or pine trees.

6. Notice one thing you can taste. Mindfully take a drink or a bite of food and slowly enjoy the experience, or imagine something yummy.

7. Finally, inhale deeply and exhale slowly, noticing how your body feels now.

Guided Meditation: Mindful and Kindful Body Scan

The first place we feel anxiety is in our bodies: a knot in the stomach, tingling in the fingers or hunched shoulders. It's different for everyone. By learning to move your attention to focus on different body parts, your mind and body connect to reduce stress and anxiety. Practising a body scan can help you recognise when you feel anxiety and release it before it becomes a full-blown panic attack. Access this guided meditation at TeachMindfulnessOnline.com/transform.

About Robyn Zagoren

Robyn is a leader in the field of wellness, with over 25 years' experience in sports medicine, ship's medicine, and health and wellness. She is the wellness coordinator for the Littleton Public School District in Colorado. Her employee wellness program has won many awards, including the American Heart Association Gold Level Workplace Health Achievement award.

www.reclaimthespark.com

4

Overcoming
Performance Anxiety

~ *Wendy Malko*

I pull into a parking spot, sweating. I start focusing on my breath. Deep breaths. Breathe in calm, breathe out peace. Or should I be breathing out tension? Ugh . . . I think I'm going to be sick.

What's that noise; is that my heart pumping? I feel like my ears are on fire. I now have anxiety ABOUT the anxiety, and that is the worst kind of anxiety.

I watch as people pass by my car. I imagine introducing myself: "Oh, hello there, nice to meet you. I'm going to be teaching your child tools to deal with anxiety today," as I casually take another breath into a paper bag.

This experience didn't happen during my first time teaching. I had a private practice where I taught mindfulness to small groups in my own space for a little over a year. Now I'd been offered an amazing opportunity to teach mindfulness to a group of children in a local psychologist's clinic. I didn't know what to expect.

Anyone who experiences performance anxiety would agree that the less you know about an event, the higher the likelihood of anxiety. I didn't know the number of children, their ages, whether there would be another person teaching with me, or what the topic was for that class. I was also asked to arrive while the group was already in session, so I would miss the first part of the class.

So, I arrived early. I sat in the parking lot, hyperventilating and thinking up all the worst-case scenarios known to man. I knew the kids would smell the anxiety on me and it would heighten their anxiety – or worse, the psychologist would sense it and would think I was a fraud. How would they ever have confidence in me if I was literally sweating through my shirt? I knew my body was in full fight-or-flight mode, and I knew that meant my brain would be offline and I wouldn't be able to access the words I needed for the class. This line of thinking brought me to the idea that maybe knowing what fight-or-flight mode does is not necessarily always that helpful in dealing with it!

That is when I started to laugh uncontrollably. The irony of it all! This group was for kids with anxiety just like mine. I was invited along to help these kids with the exact thing I was experiencing right in that moment. I needed to use the tools I was planning to share with these kids on myself, right now.

I went back to my breath: following my breath, nice and easy, all the way into my belly and all the way out. Even breaths. Breathing in and out.

I let myself feel the anxiety instead of resisting it. Resisting it only made it bigger. I let myself sit with it. I told myself it was okay to feel this way. I told myself that while some people may not have as dramatic a response as I was experiencing at that moment, feelings of anxiety are a common reaction for many people.

Then I checked in with my thoughts: just watching the thoughts, rather than getting tangled up in them. I asked myself: "What am I really afraid of?" I was thinking that I didn't have enough experience to help these kids, and that I would be seen as a fraud in front of the specialist. I questioned those thoughts. It was true, I didn't have a lot of experience in teaching mindfulness, but I had a lifetime of experience in feeling anxiety.

When I was growing up, I was referred to as shy. I remember dreading being called on in class. Even when I knew the answer was right, my lip would quiver as I spoke. I couldn't sleep at night for fear of every noise or shadow. When I was very young, I remember getting hives on my arms as we drove home from visiting people I didn't know. At the time we chalked it up to a random allergy, but looking back, I realise that my body was physically reacting to my anxiety.

As I grew older, I started allowing my anxiety to make some pretty big life decisions for me. I rationalised that I would just take one year off before going to university after graduating from high school. The truth was, I was too nervous to navigate a new school with so many strangers.

Instead, I took a job in a mental health unit within a hospital. I stayed at that job for many years, learning all that I could while working there. I read all the medical journals that were delivered to the psychiatrist at the hospital. I asked questions about mental health and the treatments that were provided. I enrolled in various distance education courses at universities, colleges and online schools in my spare time. Even though I had learnt a lot about anxiety disorders, I still didn't see how anxiety had impacted me personally.

One of my responsibilities was to field phone calls to the psychiatrist from patients in the community. Many of them had been referred to take mindfulness courses, so I decided that taking a mindfulness-based stress reduction (MBSR) course would help me better assist the patients. Meditation wasn't really my thing, but the class itself would be worth it to help the patients, and I was interested in the theory.

In that eight-week course I learnt how very wrong I had been about meditation. It wasn't until I learnt to sit and notice my thoughts and feelings, and how they felt in my body, that I finally realised how much anxiety had been ruling my life. As I sat with these emotions, they slowly began to soften.

The more time I spent on the cushion, the more I began to accept myself just as I was. In that acceptance I became passionate about sharing the tools I was learning with anyone who was experiencing the same anxiety. I kept thinking back to my childhood and how different it would have been if I'd had these tools.

I had discovered my purpose, my 'why'. It was why I continued my training to become a mindfulness teacher. It was why I accepted this opportunity to step out of my comfort zone and teach mindfulness to the children in this clinic. These kids were just like me, and they needed these tools.

I walked towards the front door of the clinic with a queasy feeling in my stomach and a racing heart, all the while reminding myself of my why.

That first session was awkward. I was so nervous that I completely forgot to connect with the kids. As I walked out of the room, I felt relieved it was over, but at the same time I felt a sense of excitement, knowing that I was learning too and it would just get easier with each opportunity.

Since then, I have been asked to speak at large gatherings at schools, businesses and various health organisations. I still get nervous, but it's a lot less awkward. I've come to realise that the discomfort in my stomach and my pounding heart are just my body's way of telling me that this is important. I have replaced the mantra of "I think I'm going to be sick," with "When I'm nervous, focus on service." Learning mindfulness has allowed me to become more aware of my anxiety and, in that awareness, I have discovered how to use my anxiety for my own growth, rather than allowing it to continue to hold me back. Mindfulness has changed my life and I am so grateful for the opportunity to share it with others.

Mindful Exercise:
Mindfully Navigating Performance Anxiety

You can apply these six tips at different stages of the process of preparing for an event, helping you to navigate the experience in a mindful and positive way.

1. When you are first invited to present or perform at an event, allow yourself to sit with any anxious feelings that arise for a moment, without pushing them away.

2. Make a list of what you need to do to prepare for the event, with dates beside each step.

3. Remind yourself to stay present during the preparation process. When you find yourself feeling anxious prior to the event, go back to your list. If there is something you need to do and you are unable to work on it in that moment, then schedule a time when you can. Take a few deep breaths and gently remind yourself that there is nothing you can do in this moment.

4. If you are having difficulty staying focused while you are working on your project, take a mindful break. Focus on your breath. Perhaps leave your workspace for some time. If you can, go outside. Spending time in nature not only has a calming effect, but it also improves attention and focus for a period afterwards.

5. Try to meditate daily for at least five to ten minutes, preferably at a time when you aren't feeling anxious. A regular practice of meditation can help calm the mind – even when you're not meditating.

6. On the day of the event, focus on your breath. Be sure to take deep, even breaths to signal to the brain that everything is okay. Keep your thoughts on the present moment. Use the time prior to the event to practise, go over notes or simply focus on your breath. It can be helpful to visualise yourself doing amazingly well during your presentation. Allow yourself to feel the pleasant thoughts of a job well done.

Guided Meditation: Public Speaking Visualisation

Calming breaths allow you to be present while you visualise yourself speaking in a group or in a difficult situation. This meditation can be particularly helpful if you experience a fear of public speaking, but it can also be beneficial prior to a job interview or important conversation. Listen to the meditation at TeachMindfulnessOnline.com/transform.

About Wendy Malko

Wendy is a mindfulness teacher and positive psychology coach. She owns the Shea Tree Wellness Center in Winnipeg, Canada, where she provides space for like-minded wellness professionals who serve their community.

www.mind-over-matter.ca

5

Overcoming Anxiety
and Encouraging Creativity

~ *Sarah Spiers*

I've experienced anxiety since I was a teenager. I remember being sat in an exam worrying about whether I'd locked the door correctly – rather than worrying about the exam!

This continued into my twenties. As a teacher, I constantly worried about not remembering dismissing a child from school, even though I always had. The excessive worry would not leave until I saw them the next day: I was unable to let go of the 'what if' scenarios. (I don't think becoming a teacher helped with my anxiety – it's stressful!)

My life changed in my mid-twenties, after I discovered mindfulness. Now, I have a better handle on my fear and anxiety. I also have a lot more books on my bookshelf, and I'm more aware of my breath, brain and body. Mindfulness is in my toolbox, along with a host of other wonderful things in my life (such as running, yoga, singing, playing the piano, chocolate cake . . .). It has helped me face my fears and given me the courage to be more resilient, and I feel as if I've expanded the limits on what I can achieve. Discovering mindfulness has also made me passionate about teaching mindfulness in schools, with the aim of equipping young people with these simple tools to use in life.

I discovered a talk on mindfulness organised by Action for Happiness, which became something I attended regularly. They invited lots of interesting speakers, facilitated engaging discussions and made me feel good after a long day. I look at my pocket-sized notebooks of inspirational things I've jotted down over the years, and lots of nuggets of wisdom came from those talks. (I recommend carrying a little notebook that fits in your pocket, so you can write down any great ideas, quotes or inspiration.)

The first mindfulness course I tried was a six-week course with The Now Project. I found it quite hard and I didn't take part in many of the discussions, but I was beginning to benefit from really focusing on the present moment. I also noticed for the first time how lovely it was to walk across a nearby bridge over the Thames. I loved crossing that bridge and looking at the buildings lit up at night while I watched the boats go by.

I discovered an online Teach Mindfulness course (with Shamash Alidina), and it immediately resonated with me. As a teacher, I find learning how to teach something is the best way to learn! Although the calming meditations sometimes sent me to sleep, I loved hearing other people's stories and liked that people were taking part from all over the world, listening and learning from each other. It was a great experience.

A component of the course involved doing a project. I knew straight away that I wanted to focus my project on mindfulness in schools. The headteacher let me do a few weeks of mindfulness with the Year 3 classes. I gave a staff talk about how we could use mindfulness in the classroom, teaching simple exercises that they could try. I bought a chime for each classroom, which ended up being a great 'one-minute refocus' mindful listening win! I went on to lead workshops for parents on mindsets and mindfulness, and I introduced them to mindful eating exercises, which they enjoyed. A parent told me how her son was using mindful breathing to calm down when he was frustrated. I found it encouraging that parents were picking up on the small changes as their children began to apply this new skill.

Running these workshops also helped me to get better at speaking in front of others. I did lots of mindful breathing beforehand and actually enjoyed standing up and talking about something that I was passionate about. We went on to achieve a Healthy Schools Silver Award based on our whole-school approach to implementing mindfulness.

One of my biggest achievements has been controlling my fear of performing music. Positive preparation helps me now. I used to always imagine the worst thing that could happen, which stopped me from doing so much. Now, rather than thinking I will forget the words, I put a lot of effort into visualising a positive outcome. It's really helped me to go out in front of an audience, sing solo and enjoy it: to be in the moment, feel my breath and go for it. I still get scared, but thanks to mindfulness I have ways to control my fear.

Mindfulness For Transformation

To me, mindfulness and the arts are entwined. They both allow you to explore your individuality. As a teacher, I am passionate about providing children with a creative education, and I would like to see mindfulness and the arts being used more to educate children about mental health: to help children to connect with each other and develop their reflective and communication skills, as well as promote curiosity and bravery.

Mindfulness has also taught me to be a lot nicer to myself. Talking to yourself as you would talk to a friend has always struck me as a helpful way to think. But probably the biggest mindfulness win for me is that it has given me so much more time to do the things I enjoy. Ruminating about my fears and anxieties on an endless loop was an absolute nightmare when I didn't have mindfulness as a tool, but now I can spend my time enjoying life rather than worrying.

I'm writing this five days before my 30th birthday, and although I would love to say that my thirties will be free of anxiety and fear, I'm realistic enough to know they won't be. Feeling anxiety is part of being human – and I think accepting that is a good thing. I hope that mindfulness is going to make a big difference to the world and allow future generations to talk openly about mental health. In hindsight, I wish I had learnt these skills earlier in my life, like the children in my school are. I hope that the 'Baby Pea' currently in my tummy is able to grow up to talk openly about the importance of looking after his brain!

I'll end with a dream for the future. I would love to open up a wellbeing café with cups of tea, cake and lots of workshops. I'd call it 'The Ripple Café', because we all go up and down like ripples on water. I hope you follow your dreams too!

Mindful Exercise:
Night-time

Waking up in the night and feeling overwhelmed, scared or worried is a feeling I know well. Your mind seems to race off so quickly, and it can leave you feeling tired and dreading the next day. Try these steps to soothe yourself and take you back to a reasonable state of mind in a few minutes.

1. **Notice:** Acknowledge your inner experience with curiosity. Step back and observe, noticing your thoughts and feelings. Turn towards any sense of discomfort and acknowledge it, without trying to change anything.

2. **Inhale:** Breathe deeply, focusing on the physical sensation of your breath. Notice the rise and fall of your body as you breathe, and try to make the exhale as long as you can until you feel back in control.

3. **Gratitude:** Bring yourself back to what you already know – what are you grateful for right now, such as the warmth of being in bed, the softness of your duvet. Breathe through the moment.

4. **Heart:** Send loving and compassionate thoughts to yourself, like those you would say to a best friend.

5. **Thought and sensation:** Scan your body for different sensations. Don't try to change them, just notice how they feel.

6. **Turn the volume down!** Don't get tangled up in your worried thoughts, because then you will form a loop of worry that will get worse. In other words, don't catastrophise. Say to yourself, "I'm just worrying" (or

create a saying that works for you). Worry isn't a new experience, but spotting it quickly and labelling it as a worry allows you to move on.

7. **Is** it true? Probably not! When you're lost in a scary scenario in your mind, label it as 'drama' and bring your attention back to the present moment. Don't let the worry develop, and don't enable your mind to exaggerate and run away beyond reality.

8. **My** anchor: Ask yourself what your anchor of focus is – for example, your breath. Come back to your anchor of focus. It will stop you from drifting too far into the story of your worry.

9. **Excitement:** Change how you look at something. You might be a little nervous about tomorrow, but fear and excitement usually come together. "Most of the really exciting things we do in our lives scare us to death. They wouldn't be exciting if they didn't." – Roald Dahl, *Danny, the Champion of the World*.

Everything is impermanent, especially worrisome situations. Accept uncertainty, relax a little and use your anchor to help you back to the land of nod.

Guided Meditation: Wake Up Fresh

This guided meditation can help you start the day off positively by taking some time to wake your body up, notice how you are feeling and encourage a positive mindset towards the day ahead. Access the audio for this meditation at TeachMindfulnessOnline.com/transform.

I must share the beautiful setting that inspired this meditation, as it's one of my favourite places to go early in the morning when I'm on holiday: Freshwater East Beach, Pembrokeshire. It's worth a visit, especially if you like watching the dogs play!

About Sarah Spiers

Sarah is a primary school music specialist teacher based in Reading. She is also an arts specialist for creative education charity Artis. She is passionate about delivering a creative education to children that integrates the performing arts through learning. She loves to sing and play the piano and enjoys performing musical theatre.

6

Finding Understanding
and Acceptance

~ *Jennifer Gilroy*

I work in a busy job. It is a good job and I enjoy it, but it can be stressful and demanding. Around five years ago, my job was at a challenging point and I was juggling quite a bit in life. But, despite all the juggling, I persevered. I thought I could work through the stressful period and come out unscathed on the other side.

Do you ever think about how sometimes society simply expects us to deal with stress: where enduring stress is considered to be a strength, and not coping with it is seen as a weakness? At the time, I didn't understand the potential damage stress could cause, or the effect it might have on me. But then I broke down. And I say I 'broke down' because not only did the experience leave me with a bad case of generalised anxiety disorder, it also made me question who I was and what I was capable of. I wound up feeling truly useless.

Then, I met Hanz, a wonderful human. He showed me how to move forward. Over time, I learnt things about myself and my past, and once I was on the mend, he introduced me to mindfulness. I was so grateful to Hanz for his support, and for introducing me to the practice of mindfulness, that I was driven to help others. And so here I am, five years later: a mindfulness teacher.

Profound things have happened to me as I have learnt about mindfulness and developed my practice: a series of insightful, transformational moments that have improved my relationship with my past experience and with the world. I will share one with you.

She

She developed terminal cancer. For nine months, I watched her fear, her sadness, her weakness, her desperate attempts to regain her health. During my five years of practising mindfulness, I had learnt what it was to sit and 'be with' all my experiences, and so I had become kinder and more forgiving. The minute I discovered the truth about her health, I decided that I wanted to spend my time learning more about her so that I could understand why life had been difficult for our family.

I discovered that she was truly wonderful. She was cheeky and, quite frankly, a pain in the behind. The nurses knew it, and so did the rest of the ward. She had a rebellious streak. She always sought freedom, although a lot of the time she couldn't reach it. I felt sadness and empathy for her continued search. She took pictures, and you could see from her social media posts that she had whisked herself away again to those comforting places of beauty. She wanted to return to those places and longed for freedom but, sometimes, she did not have the courage to find it.

She felt immense pain during her life. She lost her sister, and that's when things changed for her.

I have come to understand that she valued our relationship and considered it special – more special than I had realised. I had spent my adult years focusing on my independence and trying not to need this relationship. Then I finally understood why she had not been able to provide me with what I had needed – and I was able to forgive her.

I spent a lot of time crying on a bench at the top of a nearby hill. However, this wasn't a bad thing; it was necessary. I was grateful for my mindfulness practice, because it had opened up an empathy inside me that had previously been difficult to access. I was grateful because over those five years of developing my practice, I'd begun to see death as part of life, inevitable to us all. I knew it was okay to cry, to let the waves of emotion come and go, with no need to push them away. And I knew that what would be, would be.

At the moment she knew she was about to die, she asked us all to leave her bedside. This was the most painful feeling I have ever felt. It topped the feeling of sadness I'd had over the years, the wishing for our home life to have been different. What a final thing to do. On reflection, though, this act gives me great comfort – perhaps, even if we are scared about our own death now, we will not be so scared right at the very end. This final act encourages me to ask myself: "At the end of it all, will I have been happy? Will I have had ease of being? Will I have forgiven myself and anyone else necessary to allow us to live in harmony? Will I have felt free?" And if the answer is "No", then I work on my own wellbeing. I work a little more on developing this wonderful, peaceful presence that is growing inside me. I spend more time giving to others. I remind myself why I am teaching, and I congratulate myself for doing a good thing. I choose to pause for a while and focus more on the fun and the connection to be found in life.

The deep roots of my mindfulness practice have taught me the nature of impermanence, and I have cultivated a level of friendliness and curiosity towards my experience through my practice. You may be able to relate to why I hold mindfulness so dear – I have been able to see the difficulties in life as opportunities. The stress, the success, the suffering we experience in our attempt to 'get there', to the finish line, to the point where we can allow ourselves to stop striving and relax: none of this matters.

This is the moment that matters. This moment is all there is.

Mindful Exercise:
Moments That Matter

This practical exercise incorporates two important aspects of mindfulness: acceptance/allowing, and nourishing your own wellbeing.

1. **Spend a few minutes reflecting on what makes you happy in life, and note these down.** Try to reflect on these without feeling negative about them. For example, if you consider that 'feeling free' makes you happy, but at the moment you aren't free, this is okay. You don't need to reflect on the reasons why you don't feel free, simply list what makes you happy.

2. **Now, list the things that would bring about this sense of happiness.** Try to list the small and the big things. For example, perhaps a walk by the sea by yourself makes you feel free. Maybe climbing a mountain brings different feelings of freedom.

3. **Pick one thing that you could do soon.** It doesn't have to be something difficult to achieve (like climbing a mountain); instead, consider something that you can carry out in the next month or so, such as a walk by your local river.

4. **Do this one thing.** Pay attention to how you feel when you do it, and let these feelings nourish you.

5. **Make a point of doing this thing more.** Give yourself permission to find more moments of happiness. Go wild with your list!

Guided Meditation: Peaceful Freedom in Nature

Connecting with nature can be a peaceful experience. In this guided meditation, I take you on a soothing guided visualisation journey into nature. Listen to the guided meditation at TeachMindfulnessOnline.com/transform.

About Jennifer Gilroy

Jen is a mindfulness teacher based in Surrey, England.

www.zenjen-mindfulliving.co.uk

7

Using Mindfulness to Cope with Grief

~ Jane Bozier

I was in my twenties when I lost a baby, very unexpectedly and very traumatically. Not only did I lose my baby, I lost any chance of ever having another one, and what followed was a downward spiral of depression fuelled by loss, anger, darkness and despair.

My grief became my private internal space, which I shared with no one. I had a child already, and for a while I lost sight of her. I was consumed by such dark thoughts and feelings that they held me in a place with no hope, no answers and no future.

The conventional medical model of treatment was offered to me. I took antidepressants and had counselling, but I felt they were all in vain because nothing was going to bring my baby back.

The weight of the world that I had built around my loss was so heavy. I contemplated suicide; I didn't really want to die, but I was just too tired to carry on living. I got everything ready, but just as I was about to go through with it, my daughter woke up and called out for me. I knew, in that moment, that I had to change – and so began my self-help journey.

I read book after book after book. I studied counselling. My self-help quest occasionally gave me bits and pieces of hope in the form of yoga, meditation and aromatherapy that I didn't really understand but seemed to make a difference and complemented the medication that I was taking. However, nothing filled the hole in my heart or replaced the emptiness. I knew that I had to find a way of living with what had happened.

I was in my forties when I was given a book called *The Mindful Way Through Depression* by Mark Williams, John Teasdale, Zindel Segal and Jon Kabat-Zinn. I didn't read it, I just put the CD on every night and listened to the body scan. At the time, I thought it was a load of rubbish but, for some unknown reason, I kept going. I can't say exactly how or why, but that feeling of being exactly where I was meant to be happened one night during the body scan. The invading thoughts that had haunted me for so many years were quietened each time I gently escorted my mind back to my body. A glimmer of hope arose.

I read the book and listened to some more of the CD; this time, the sitting meditation. With patience and practice, I noticed how much my mind wandered and how frequently the same thoughts arose. I noticed that I was caught on a hamster wheel of hopelessness, but paying attention to my breath seemed to help stop the spinning. This sparked my interest even more, so I signed up for a four-session mindfulness course online, which led to a five-day retreat where I completed a mindfulness-based stress reduction (MBSR) course. I felt as if all my searching had led me to mindfulness. It had prepared me for this exact moment, and I was ready.

It was not an easy journey. So many of the thoughts and feelings that I had denied myself and hidden from others were surfacing, but I didn't feel frightened anymore. It was such a relief to watch my thoughts pass over my head like clouds – it really did ease my mind. I stopped trying to suppress my thoughts, which had been taking up so much of my energy. It didn't fill the emptiness that had long been a part of my life, but it did help me to walk side by side with my loss for the first time, to accept it as being a part of me – a part of me, but not the whole of me.

My daily practice helped me to learn more about myself, to understand that being kind to myself is okay and that what happened to me was out of my control. It didn't happen because I was a bad person. There is no rhyme or reason for life's events. Acceptance and letting things be have given me back my life – and, more importantly, my daughter – and for that I am grateful. My mental health has become my friend, not my foe. It is a part of the jigsaw of my life, one part of the complexity of being me, and when I am having a crisis, I understand that nothing is permanent. It will change, my thoughts are okay, they are not me. I'm not saying that dealing with a crisis isn't an unpleasant experience, because it is. It's such a dark place to sit. However, it lasts for less time now.

Grief turned my life upside down, leading me to depression. Mindfulness turned my life back upright; it centred me, and I felt I could breathe again. It found me 12 years ago – drawing together the small nuggets of hope that I had clung to throughout my adult life – and it clicked, made sense and changed everything. I am no longer controlled by my negative internal thoughts, and as a result

I am more awake to the pleasant times. I have become more aware that most of my days are neutral, neither pleasant nor unpleasant, but each day gives me some moments of joy and happiness.

My mindfulness journey has given me so many opportunities, and I have met some wonderful people. I find there is always something to be grateful for and to smile about, especially my daughter and my grandchildren. I have realised that unpleasant moments are few and far between, and the majority of them are due to my choices anyway; they are my doing. I don't get as stressed about the unpleasant moments that are not down to my choices – the things I cannot control. Instead, I do a three-minute breathing space meditation and carry on regardless.

I love to just breathe, to count each in-breath and each out-breath, especially when I am lying in bed. I have sand timers and snow globes in each room, which act as visual reminders for me to pause at different times during the day for mindful moments. I love to smell the roses or freshly-brewed coffee, and I'm once again able to see the beauty among the chaos.

I spent so many years lost because I lived in the past and the future. I'm never lost with mindfulness to hand. It grounds me in the present by giving me mindful moments. I'm not lost anymore: I'm able to pause and be still.

Mindful Exercise:
Pause for a Mindful Minute

This exercise shows you the number of breaths that you take in one minute. Before you start, a gentle reminder: there is no right or wrong number of breaths, and you do not have to change your breathing – just breathe naturally.

1. Find a quiet space and set a timer or alarm for one minute.
2. Close your eyes and count your breaths – each in-breath and out-breath counts as one breath.
3. Stop counting once the timer or alarm rings.
4. You now know the number of breaths that you take in one minute. If it helps to remember, write down the number in a diary, notebook or on your phone.

Your individual number of breaths is a tool to give you an opportunity to pause for a mindful minute at any point, day or night. All you need to do is close your eyes and count that number of breaths.

Guided Meditation: Body Scan

This guided body scan meditation can help your mind and body to relax as you move your attention from your feet through your body. You can access the meditation at TeachMindfulnessOnline.com/transform.

About Jane Bozier

Jane is a registered mental health nurse with 35 years' experience. She has a master's degree in mindfulness and has been practising and teaching mindfulness for 10 years. She regularly writes articles about mindfulness, mental health, sleep and other areas of health and wellbeing.

8

Slowing Down with Mindfulness: A Route to Whole-body Wellbeing

~ Annabel Deans

The death of my beloved mum in 2007 had a massive impact on me. I watched as she battled courageously against the rare, painful autoimmune disease that would eventually consume her at just 67. She had been a nurse in our local hospital for 45 years, where she devoted her life to caring for others. So, the tables had turned: she was in a nursing home, where she was in need of constant care herself. It was so hard to watch her deteriorate and feel unable to make her better.

At the time, I had a toddler and a baby. I was exhausted from sleepless nights and the constant demands on my time and attention. I lived on autopilot. I suppose deep down I knew what was coming, but I couldn't comprehend it. I was being pulled mindlessly forward, edging slowly towards the abyss. I felt a huge array of emotions. There was frustration and anger: why was this happening to her? Guilt: was I visiting her enough, while also trying to be with my young family? Was I being a good enough mother to my children? Could they detect my frame of mind and deep-rooted sadness? I felt jealous of my friends enjoying family life with their own mothers, when I couldn't. I didn't like the feelings that were arising within me and I often felt lonely, yet my coping strategies were limited. Wasn't it best just to sweep it all under the carpet? Wouldn't I be happier if I didn't think about any of it and just got on with being a busy young mum?

After the initial grief of Mum's death, which blindsided me, that's exactly what I did. I packed all my natural emotions away in a small cupboard in the back of my mind. But my body hadn't forgotten, and that emotional pain found a way to present itself. The next decade was a whirlwind. I felt like I was in a permanent hurry, with my stress levels sky-high. I talked fast, I sped everywhere and I was quick to anger because I felt overwhelmed. I went to see a coach, who told me in no uncertain terms to slow down if I wanted to achieve my goals. Those words struck like an arrow deep in my heart: there was so much truth in them.

Physically, my digestion was bad, my stomach was bloated and I had developed an allergic reaction to random foods that left my face swollen and my legs covered in hives. I visited a nutritionist who helped me, and this sparked an interest within me: I wanted to know how to have as healthy a body as possible. This was in part fuelled by a fear that what had happened to Mum could happen to me. I started to change my diet, but a part of the puzzle was still missing.

I attended a vision board workshop run by a friend who was a health coach. Sitting with a group of strangers, I stuck pictures onto a whiteboard of things I wanted to manifest in my life that year. To be honest, I was a bit sceptical. Towards the end of the workshop, I asked where she had studied, and that night I looked up the course. This was it! A sudden decisiveness overtook me and two days later I had enrolled.

The course took a holistic view of health: it considered the person as a whole as well as nutrition. I was introduced to the mind-body connection for the first time. It was a lightbulb moment. I'd practised yoga for many years, so I was aware of the power of the breath, but the lectures on the science behind mindfulness and its myriad benefits were eye-opening. I listened to many different teachers and began reading more about mindfulness. The changes in me were subtle at first: I hadn't reacted to a certain situation in the way I would normally; I was more patient and less stressed. If I just paused, I could respond rather than react. Wow! That was a revelation. I'd never realised there was a choice before!

Could my state of mind have a positive impact on my body? Well, the intense tension headaches were much less frequent. I could keep my endless ruminating in check. I was sleeping well and, if I did struggle, I would follow a breathing technique and it would help me to drift off. I began to radiate a new-found energy that people would often comment upon.

A wonderful by-product of my practice is that I have finally slowed down! I take the time to walk in nature and to really listen to the birds singing, the leaves rustling and the crunch of twigs under my feet. I pause to smell the roses in my garden and appreciate the lovely corner of England in which I live: all the things I had been just too busy to pay attention to before. My mind feels clearer, and there's more room for creativity. Perhaps it was my freshly acquired focus that helped all the things on my vision board to come true in the end!

But the best thing of all is that I've realised it's okay to feel negative emotions. I can open that dusty cupboard in the back of my mind and take a look inside. I can accept what's there with kindness and just let those emotions be present. And when I acknowledge them in this way, their power over me fades. I feel so blessed to be starting on this new career in mindfulness in my late forties and to have discovered a new way of approaching life. It really feels like a gift from above: I like to think my mum had something to do with it, and I love passing this gift on to others.

Mindfulness is about the journey, not the destination, and I have come to accept that my path has been a long and meandering one. I'm still travelling along it daily, but with a lot more awareness than before. I now know how to greet whatever I find on this path with an open heart and with a lot more compassion.

I am so grateful for this new understanding of the connection between my mind and my body, each one working more in harmony with the other through my mindfulness practice. Over time, small changes can make a big impact on your life. Remember: every journey starts with a single step, and I am proof that it is never too late to start. The best moment is the present moment!

Mindful Exercise:
A Handy Pause

This exercise is a mindful moment to press the pause button and reconnect your body and mind before you continue with your day.

1. Find a comfortable seated position and pinch the thumb and index finger of one hand together. Take a deep inhale and a long exhale. Look carefully at your hand and notice the patterns on your knuckles, the lines on your palm and the veins just beneath the surface. Is your skin rough or smooth?

2. Pinch your thumb and middle finger together and take a deep inhale and long exhale and notice any sensations in your hands. Is there a pulsing or a tingling sensation? Is your hand hot or cold?

3. Pinch your thumb and ring finger together. Gently close your eyes and take a deep inhale and long exhale. What are you thinking? Try not to judge your thoughts; just imagine them flowing like a stream of energy to your fingertips and then floating away into the air.

4. Pinch your thumb and little finger together. With your eyes still closed, notice any emotions. Perhaps label them: stress, anxiety, tiredness. Breathe into these feelings and just let them rest in your awareness without any judgement.

5. Finally, press each finger against your thumb in turn and think of one thing you are grateful for today. Congratulate yourself for taking the time to nourish your body and mind in this moment.

Repeat daily or whenever you need to, and note any insights in your journal.

Guided Meditation: Permission to Slow Down

After a busy day, it can be difficult to slow down, press the pause button and make time for yourself. This meditation presents you with an opportunity to slow down and find peace in the present moment. Listen to the guided meditation at TeachMindfulnessOnline.com/transform.

About Annabel Deans

Annabel lives in rural Kent and is a married mum of teenage boys. She is a holistic health coach and mindfulness teacher and runs Be Well with Annabel. She adores cooking Greek food, walking the dog in the woods, reading, playing golf and practising Qi Gong. You can contact her on hello@bewellwithannabel.co.uk.

9

Settling into Stillness, Returning to Wholeness

~ *Carol Hickson*

All my life I had felt untethered and irrelevant. No matter how hard I tried, the ground always slipped from under me.

By the time I reached 50 in 2013, I had been exhausted for years. My marriage of 23 years had ended. My partner from my second relationship had died in my arms from a brain tumour and, five years later, history repeated itself when my dad died in my arms.

Here, I share some of the significant experiences which taught me that I alone can be the change in my own life.

I am the youngest child of alcoholic parents. My mother never acknowledged the damage that her addiction and years of drunken behaviour caused to our family. Our fragile world, built on eggshells, centred around her.

On 5th November 2012, the fifth anniversary of my partner's cremation, my dad was diagnosed with cancer of the oesophagus.

I was so proud of him and the way he received the prognosis. He was very kind to the nurse delivering the news: "Please don't be upset for me, I've lived my life in the way I chose." He died the following January.

I had always been a poor sleeper, and his death worsened my insomnia; I was sleeping for only an hour a night. Later, during therapist training, I discovered that my subconscious mind had linked my bereavements to sleep: if you fall asleep, you die.

There were glimmers of hope amongst the darkest grey: two of my children graduated and started their careers, my youngest child started at university, I bought a house with my new partner, and I graduated and was accepted onto a full-time PGCE teaching course in modern foreign languages (after which I became a teacher). The chaos of my sleep, however, meant that every day was harder than the last. It had deteriorated to the point where, as well as only sleeping for an hour, I was having night terrors.

Neither counselling nor the medical profession could help. I was on medication to try to reset my circadian rhythm, but powerful drugs had no effect; I remained wide awake.

I spent my savings on holistic therapists, counsellors and private specialists. Occasionally, they lifted me, but there was always the unstable relationship with my mother to set me back again. With every bitter onslaught from her, a part of me unravelled as it always had since my childhood.

In late 2016, I experienced a series of difficult events that would see me reach breaking point. As well as the uncertainty of Mum's behaviour and the sleep deprivation, I was struggling with the workload of a newly qualified teacher, plus the chronic pain of three prolapsed discs in my lumbar region, for which I held a disabled blue badge. In September, the left side of my face fell, and I lost both the ability to smile and my yawn reflex. A few weeks later I lost the strength in my left arm and hand, and was convinced I was having a stroke.

The results from an MRI scan were delivered on 19th December 2016 and came at the start of a Christmas week that was to change my life forever.

The consultant told me that I needed surgery to replace two discs in my neck. I left the appointment in a haze of ambiguity. Someone was finally being proactive in a way that might help me, and yet neck surgery felt like a bad fit.

I telephoned my mother, hoping that she would support me. I shared my fears of paralysis and exhaustion, and at the time she was encouraging and kind. But, three hours later I received a stack of drunken answer-machine messages of the foulest nature from her.

Two days later, when she was sober, I telephoned her and played her messages back. I recorded the call so that she couldn't fabricate any more lies. I told her that I loved her, but that I could no longer tolerate her behaviour towards my children and me. I explained that should she wish to call and be pleasant then I would be delighted to hear from her, but that we could no longer continue like this. I was shaking but relieved when I put the phone down – finally, I had found my courage and voiced my truth. I was calm, honest and kind to her, and I hoped that this would move our relationship to a better place.

The next day, an uninsured driver shunted into my partner's car. Due to whiplash, I was left unemployed. Two days later, on Christmas Day, my brother found our mother dead at her home. I phoned an auntie on the 27th December to tell her about Mum, and she told me that her husband, a favourite uncle, had died on Boxing Day. I truly felt as if the sky had fallen in. During the course of one week, the landscape of my life had been redrawn.

It felt as if I was embroiled in a fight for survival but I knew I had to persist, and so I enrolled on a short mindfulness course (with Shamash Alidina). It was hard – I was so used to the battering ram of my own inner critic that being kind towards myself was anathema to me.

However, in the days following Mum's death, I felt as if a weight had been lifted. Initially, I felt guilty admitting this, but I now accept that this is my truth. One difficulty in growing up with a parent who treats you badly is the conflict of emotion. The voice of survival tells you to walk away, but hope is eternal – and so I had clung on, waiting for her to change. When I was finally able to set my boundary, two days before her death, it was for my own survival.

A few months later, I slept for five hours for the first time in years. The battle with the night terrors has been harder fought, but slowly the loops in my brain have been unravelling. The unwavering support of my family has helped me to see myself through a fairer filter and to slowly develop a sense of safety.

Mindfulness and the Emotional Freedom Technique (EFT) have helped me to accept what is. I no longer need a blue badge; I have no numbness or pain. I avoided having an operation after all. My futile fight for approval is over. Quieting my chattering monkey brain has been altogether harder, but I refuse to be diverted. When the carousel of critical thoughts attempts to subvert me, I persevere with self-compassionate kindness.

People who know me well tell me that I am the kind person they have always known. It would appear the fight was only in my head after all. The 16-year-old me was very much as I am now – spiritual and compassionate – and I realise that after a 40-year detour I have returned to myself.

After so many years of poor programming, I choose to be mindful of my thoughts because choice is a gift. Each day I choose to be grateful: I have my partner, my children, good friends and a fulfilling career. I am mentally resilient and strong. Without the constant derogation, I like myself more and more. Each day I settle deeper into stillness, returning to the me who waited patiently in the wings of life's dramas. I find myself content.

As I write this, I wouldn't change a thing. At times, I miss my parents, and I believe they did the best they could with what they had. I have no doubt that in their own way they loved me, but they were both overwhelmed by their own histories and by the distorted filter of alcohol. My experiences have moulded and formed me into the person I am, and for that I am grateful.

Within each of us lies a kernel of possibility for change that once acknowledged and nurtured, can help us as we actively overcome our negative thoughts and interrupt our limiting patterns of behaviour. This, I believe, is how we transform.

Mindful Exercise:
Reconnecting with Stillness

If you find yourself caught in a loop of anxiety and worry, this exercise – using bilateral stimulation, which involves using both sides of the brain – will untangle your thoughts and move you into the present.

1. Place your hands together lightly in a prayer position. Feel the gentle pressure as your fingertips and palms touch. Be aware of the lightness of that touch, like the breath of an infant or the stroke of a feather, and very, very slowly begin to slide your hands up and down against each other. Gently begin to connect the tips of your fingers, the hollow palm of your hand, your thumb. The parts of you that are unique to you – just like every snowflake is unique.

2. Look at the palms of your hands. Notice the etched lines: the love line and the life line, the routes of who you are and who you can become. The story of who you are is engraved upon your fingertips and palms.

3. Become aware of the energy building in this connection between your hands. Slowly, explore the lines, the contours of your skin and fingertips, discovering this unique landscape of you and every possibility that awaits you. Notice the subtle shades of the skin on your hands. Notice yourself noticing these variations.

4. You may like to gently rub your hands together with your eyes closed. Begin to interrupt the habits of your tangled mind, instilling calm as you reconnect with the sense of touch, of the energy passing between your hands – the sense of you. Settle into the stillness which is you.

Use this exercise to help ground you and to remind yourself of your uniqueness and your physical presence.

Guided Meditation: Settling into Stillness

This guided meditation follows the theme of reconnection. Many anxious people lose their connection with themselves. This grounding or centering forms the foundations of healing. Listen to the meditation at <u>TeachMindfulnessOnline.com/transform</u>.

About Carol Hickson

Carol lives in Cheshire, in the North West of England. She is a multi-disciplined therapist and mindfulness teacher helping others to navigate their detours, find ways to reframe their stories and make the most of being alive. Cozumel, Carol's trainee therapy dog, helps too!

www.carolhickson.co.uk

Part II:

Discovering the
Transformative Power of
Mindfulness, Compassion
and Self-compassion

10

From Breakdown
to Breakthrough

~ John Danias

I grew up in a stable family. I valued happiness and aspired to structure a life that supported my interests as they changed over time. I loved surfing and lived by the sea. In my thirties, as my peers were climbing the career and affluence ladder, I moved to London and into finance. It was interesting and it gave me financial peace of mind, which eliminated many stresses.

Over time, however, my confidence and happiness began to erode. I was juggling more work than I was comfortable with, and felt that everyone else was smarter than me, which diminished my confidence and dulled my mind. However, I had a family to support, so I felt that living a dull, grey life was a price worth paying. I was stuck on the perpetual treadmill of the rat race. My mind was too foggy to see the exit sign, let alone the wider world outside.

One night in February 2013, I woke up at 2am feeling as if my mind had split; specifically, my emotional state and sense of logic seemed to have split. It's hard to describe. One moment I was crying while not feeling sad, then I was laughing while feeling nothing . . . and many other bizarre combinations. It reminded me of a cartoon car hurtling down the road, wheels falling off and spinning independently alongside as it headed for a crash. My mind had split in two and there was nothing holding the pieces together. I was dysfunctional, out of control. I had broken down. I thought this would be my new reality.

Thankfully, only an hour later, my mind gelled back together again. The cogs, pistons and pipes all linked up – I was functional, roadworthy. I could move within the structure of everyday life without crashing. I felt very lucky.

I was back to normal, yet something had changed. I felt gratitude for the precious gift of simply being functional and in one piece. I felt wonder at the intricacy of my mind and the way its myriad parts were working coherently together.

I became particularly interested in exploring my internal landscape, like an explorer or scientist uncovering new terrain. By familiarising myself with 'the stuff that John is made of' – the interplay of thoughts and emotions, responses to sensory inputs, my breath, my body – I developed a better understanding of my internal landscape. I had dabbled with mindfulness and other mind-training techniques in the past, and now it became my vocation.

Over time, I became less caught up in ruminating about the past and stressing about the future. The negative thoughts continued, but their charge had weakened. Rather than being immersed in my thoughts, I learnt to observe them as if watching a movie. Worries about having less income to support my family lost their emotional charge. The fear disappeared. Clarity had been restored.

I started believing in myself: not the 'I will be a success' type of belief, but something deeper. Something beyond triumph and failure, joy and suffering – something I cannot explain with logic. It's like walking with full conviction into a deep but gradually clearing mist, with no idea of your destination.

I began dedicating time to doing the things that I love, knowing that they nourish me and that I show up better for my family and my work. I gradually lost the fear of coming across as foolish at work, and this has brought with it more confidence. Redundancy came up at my previous job and, with my wife's support, we welcomed it as an opportunity for a new adventure. After 19 years in London, we moved to Newbury, a small town where our son could attend a more suitable secondary school.

For me, mindfulness is about consciously bringing awareness to the experience at hand. I don't see it as binary – being mindful or not – but rather greyscale. Being more detached from my thoughts, more present, more curious, even by one per cent, seems worthwhile. I have become particularly fascinated with cultivating mindful qualities through daily activities, be it walking to the shops, cooking at home or negotiating at work. I also love the huge crossover between mindfulness and other mind-training practices such as neurofeedback, hypnotherapy, transformational breathing and even free diving.

Life is not as fixed as I believed; it is not just good or bad, but a cocktail. Now, I'm feeling positive. I'm more conscious of the ingredients of my experience and tuned in to the dance of life.

Is it right to view life through an optimistic lens? When faced with a query like that, I think the wiser question to ask is, "Is it helpful?" Well today, as I'm writing, I feel the answer is yes.

Mindful Exercise:
An Energising Mindful Walk

In my experience, insights arising through mindfulness practice tend to occur in unexpected moments within everyday life. So it is helpful to cultivate mindfulness within daily activities as well as while sitting in a quiet room.

I like to do this exercise when going for a walk, although it can be adapted to any activity. The premise is to become less caught up in your thoughts and more engaged with the present moment, by bringing attention to your sensory experience.

1. Before leaving your home or office, take a moment to notice your posture. Imagine there is a thread pulling you up from the top of your head while another thread is pulling down at your feet. Stretch, but remain comfortable – expanded and loose.

2. Stepping outside, bring awareness to the sensation of your feet: notice the changing degree and location of pressure as you move.

3. Tune in to the soundscape: receive the sounds around you.

4. Tune in to the visual field: receive the light around you. In particular, be aware of what is not directly in front of you without turning your head.

5. Let go of any intention and permit your mind to do its own thing. This is a gradual transition: let go of the instructions gently while continuing with your activity, so that the meditative practice blends into everyday life.

This is an active meditation, so the main focus remains the task at hand; for example, the walk to the train station or the shops. The mindful walking experience is secondary and should remain in the background – letting the steps above stay in the background is enough. With practice, you become more attuned to walking mindfully effortlessly, like learning how to drive a car or ride a bike.

Guided Meditation: Mindful Walking

You might like to try the mindful walking exercise above as a guided meditation. I recommend that you try it when you're not in a rush. After a couple of times, experiment with the duration and instructions – most importantly, drop any expectations and have fun with it! Listen to the guided meditation at TeachMindfulnessOnline.com/transform.

About John Danias

John lives in the UK and shares his time between his family, his work (in real estate finance) and exploring mindfulness in the context of everyday life.

www.mindfulexperiences.co.uk

11

How Lockdown Helped Me Find Greater Harmony

~ Lauretta Mazza

I have been practising and teaching mindfulness for many years, but I felt it really changed my life during the coronavirus pandemic lockdown.

Italy was one of the first countries to be hit by the pandemic, and in the beginning no one knew what it would lead to. We were asked to stay at home, avoid social connections, and only go out for the bare essentials, such as buying food or walking the dog; nothing more.

Suddenly, we all had a lot of time to fully live in the present moment, to just be. It was like watching a slow motion action replay, or experiencing a significant moment in your life when you can perceive and register all the details of that moment like a perfect photograph. The slow motion of the new reality amplified the sense that I was alive, tuning me deeply into my breathing, the sensation of walking, the feeling of the water while washing my hands.

I recalled a similar feeling of being present from my childhood when, during long holidays in the mountains with 'nothing' to do, I would find myself reading, walking, creating new games and telling stories with the other children and laughing about every little thing.

The key of transformation was given to me when I found all that time in lockdown – the gift of time to be in the present moment, without running towards a goal.

I am lucky to live with a dog and a cat, surrounded by books and flowers. My first response to the new reality was to move the furniture of my little apartment and create a space for mindful movement. I found the tripod for my mobile and subscribed to video conferencing so that I could continue teaching my mindful movement classes online.

Only a few students faced the challenge with me, but those who did have never abandoned this new mode of attending classes. Like me, they have learned to use new technologies and maximise their potential. My days soon became full thanks to these technologies, as students, friends and family members appeared on the screen to spend time with me, while the days passed without us knowing what tomorrow would bring.

My slow, conscious walks inside the apartment marked the different hours of the day. From this space on the carpet, close to my books, I could admire the beautiful panorama from my window: the village walls, the nearby town, the green hills dotted with farmhouses. I had created a special space to return to, one in which I could find kindness and acceptance – a space infused with the curiosity of a new meeting. These experiences started to feel like magical moments, and this space called out to me several times during the day.

The hypersensitivity that has always accompanied me gave way to change, to acceptance. The suspended time of the first month of lockdown flowed away quickly, but the second month and the subsequent weeks of continued confinement presented me with an opportunity to go deep into my practice and discover – or rediscover – how to let go of the habits, attitudes and behaviours brought about by living on autopilot. I was simply at home, in my practice, into being.

Even now, on the resumption of all activities – the open-air classes and the daily walks in nature – the magical space I created at home, where everything happened for so long, hasn't disappeared. It has become more solid and important to me: it helps me to know myself, accept myself, to be with myself in a totally new way. Practising meditation more often than usual seems to have given me access to a new door, a new entrance, a new dimension of being, where everything is more harmonious.

Every time I get close to the magic carpet, close to the books on my shelves, the quality of my day becomes brighter, more brilliant.

My mindfulness adventure continues as a source of precious discoveries that lead to a special path into being – all starting from the sound of a bell.

Mindful Exercise:
Coming Home to Your Body

These three simple steps help you to come home to your body, wherever and whenever you want to centre your body, mind and spirit.

1. Stand with your feet hip-width apart, and start to shift your body very slowly from side to side.
2. Connect to your breath.
3. Put the tip of your tongue to your upper palate, behind your incisors, and relax your jaw.

Keep doing these three things for a couple of minutes and notice how you feel more present, calm and aligned.

Guided Meditation: Light Body Scan

This version of the body scan meditation uses an imagined light to illuminate the body and calm the mind. Listen to the guided audio meditation at <u>TeachMindfulnessOnline.com/transform</u>.

About Lauretta Mazza

Lauretta is a Trager practitioner, and she teaches the Franklin Method, NIA Moving to Heal, restorative yoga and mindfulness. She runs courses for individuals, companies, communities and small groups in both Italian and English. Lauretta lives in Tuscany, Italy.

www.in-movimento.org/eng
www.trager.it

12

Discovering the Power of Self-compassion

~ Dana Abou Zeki

When I started practising meditation a couple of years ago, I was a complete emotional wreck. I was struggling with overthinking and feeling overwhelmed. I remember crying so much during my meditation training, unable to control my emotions, and most of my questions were about suffering, acceptance and letting go. I wanted answers to all the questions I had in my mind – questions about life, suffering, my path and my true purpose – but mostly I wanted a guarantee that I could trust in the stillness to make me feel better, and that meditation was going to heal the broken parts of me and put me back together.

Overthinking can silently paralyse your life and lead to severe depression. When you overthink, you can get caught up in past events and your thoughts become facts. This overthinking state can lead people to befriend their suffering, especially if it feels that it is the only thing they can control. My overthinking mind sadly turned my autopilot operating mode into a bittersweet certainty, which became a safe zone that distracted me from how much my thoughts were affecting my health, my feelings and my life.

I was the person at the end of a yoga class who could not lie still in Shavasana, not even for a few seconds, while others easily relaxed into the posture. It took me some time to realise why this was happening. I was trying so hard, and I thought that I just didn't have the ability to relax my body and mind; the truth, however, was different. I was simply afraid! Afraid to be left alone with my thoughts and feelings as they started to strongly surface from the safe zone I had hidden them in the minute my body hit the ground. Stillness was forcing me to face what I had successfully hidden deep down inside for many years.

It was only through the consistent practice of meditation that I began to slowly have the courage to sit with my emotions and pain, accept my feelings and experiences, and start to release the layers of fear that were holding me back.

Mindfulness training opened my mind and heart to more opportunities for presence. I learnt new awareness techniques and practices that deepened and changed my sense of stillness and awareness, giving me more freedom to exercise my 'muscle' of awareness throughout each day. I started noticing the simple pleasures in life, like the clouds in the sky and the many shades of colour in a sunset, the sound of birds and the feeling of the ground beneath my feet. I felt happier and lighter knowing that I could simply disconnect for a minute and feel at peace with myself anywhere, simply by following my breath and consciously connecting with it.

The practice of mindfulness helped me cultivate the awareness that I needed to make room for change in my life. I learnt to accept what I couldn't change and work on changing what I could. I started to observe my thoughts and emotions more closely, while allowing myself to feel them fully, and then I learnt to witness them with non-judgement, non-attachment and, most importantly, with compassion.

Self-compassion is something that I didn't believe existed within me. I was hard on myself, seeking perfection while rooted in my fears of not being good enough and my doubts about the direction of my life. But the more I practised mindfulness, the kinder I became towards myself, my thoughts, my emotions and my body.

Teaching mindfulness has been such a rewarding element on my path of self-discovery, as it allowed me to connect and feel deeply with others as well as myself. I realised that we all have similar sufferings, they're just covered in different skins. I found that self-compassion was lacking in so many people, so in my Mindfulness for Stress courses I teach, I do my best to focus on helping others cultivate self-compassion within themselves. I truly believe that self-compassion is the foundation for change and growth. The more I teach, the more I learn about and value human connection, kindness and compassion.

Stress affects people differently, and mindfulness can help us to cultivate a deeper level of self-awareness that enables us to manage our stress and make the changes we need to make in our lives. It is through our mindful self-awareness that we begin to understand and feel how stress affects our bodies, our minds and our behaviours, allowing us to notice what triggers our stress and when our stress levels start to rise. We learn to acknowledge and feel our emotions fully and not deny or run away from them. We begin to slowly start learning how to confront our own feelings in a gentle, compassionate and more mindful way. Mindfulness can help us to identify the patterns of thoughts and behaviours that no longer serve us, which clears space within us for overcoming stress, making wiser decisions and cultivating self-compassion.

Mindfulness has helped me to grow as a person and a teacher. It has given me the gift of self-compassion, which I believe can be genuinely transformative. I am truly grateful.

Mindful Exercise:
Dealing with Lingering Emotions

This exercise can help you learn how to sit with your emotions, so you are able to deal with and release them.

1. Find a comfortable and quiet space.

2. Close your eyes, and take slow and deep breaths in and out of your nose or mouth to centre and ground yourself.

3. Gently bring to mind an emotional situation or an intense feeling you have experienced.

4. Notice if that brings about any thoughts, images or bodily sensations – as if that situation or intense feeling is happening now. How does that affect your feelings? Are they more intense? Label your emotions.

5. Notice where you are feeling the emotions in the body. Be curious in your exploration, yet also non-judgemental and gentle.

6. Sit with your emotions and start to slowly breathe through your experience, allowing your awareness to shift to the flow and sensation of your breath. Every time your mind wanders, or you feel a stronger emotion, take a deeper breath in to gently draw the attention back to the flow and sensation of your breath.

7. Allow the breath to calm you down. Give yourself permission to release your lingering emotions. Maybe repeat out loud or in your mind a few times, "I give myself permission to fully release my emotions." Treat your emotions like waves in the ocean, coming and going, and

stay connected to your breath as you slowly start to release them.

8. Gently open your eyes.

Remember to always be kind, gentle and compassionate with yourself. If you feel overwhelmed with your emotions, conclude the exercise and take a few calming breaths – you may find that you can return to this practice another time.

Guided Meditation: Mindfulness for Difficult Emotions

This meditation aims to help you to release difficult emotions in a mindful way. Listen to the guided meditation at TeachMindfulnessOnline.com/transform.

About Dana Abou Zeki

Dana is based in Beirut, Lebanon. She is a certified mindfulness coach and a meditation and yoga teacher, and she offers online one-to-one coaching via Zoom and Google Meet. She spreads wellness, happiness and health by teaching mindfulness techniques that help others to manage and decrease their stress levels and live a more balanced life.

www.mindfulvedana.com

13

Becoming Inspired to Take a New Path in Life

~ *Susan Haigh*

As I approached my mid-forties, my lifestyle didn't include anything spiritual. Terms such as 'mindfulness' and 'holistic therapies' weren't part of my vocabulary: I'd worked from the age of 16, holding down a variety of jobs while getting married and starting a family. All that changed when a dear friend of mine was diagnosed with terminal cancer.

During her last couple of months, as part of her treatment, she tried a range of holistic therapies, including reiki, meditation and gentle massage. I clearly recall her saying, "Susan, this is something you must try."

I found myself feeling restless in my own life: my son was growing up quickly, and my job wasn't fulfilling. However, I wasn't sure what I was looking for.

One evening, on my drive home from work as the car sat stationary at the traffic lights, my attention was drawn to a poster advertising a ten-week holistic therapy course at a local college. I remembered my friend's words and how much she had benefited from the power of living in the moment: she was an inspiration to me, so brave and happy. As the evening progressed, I kept thinking about the poster.

The next day, out of curiosity, I called in to the centre and decided to enrol on the course. Why not? It was only ten weeks, after all. The course was something I had never experienced before. I learnt about massage, breathing techniques, visualisation, as well as talking about thoughts and feelings. I knew I had found the future path I'd been looking for. I was about to embark on a wonderful journey.

I left my job and enrolled on a two-year, full-time holistic therapy course. I started reading books on various therapies, and mindfulness. I was hooked. The further I dived into the reading, the deeper my understanding of living in the present moment became, which guided me in all areas of my life: my studies, my home life and my experiences in the wider world. My learning moved me beyond the words on the pages alone – I was learning just as much within myself.

After I qualified, I started to work on a voluntary basis, offering massage care and support at a hospice for those undergoing treatment for cancer. I met some incredible people during that time, and I truly felt I had found my calling.

Over the next seven years, I developed as a therapist while working at a couple of spas. I was living life mindfully, with an appreciation of my health and everyone and everything around me. Eventually, I took a big leap and decided to work for myself, as I had an evolving vision of how different treatments could help people.

People come to me not only for help managing their physical aches and pains, but also to boost their mental, spiritual and emotional wellbeing. Although I don't teach mindfulness, I introduce it into my therapies and I share it with my friends and family.

I truly believe that the universe is guiding me and will also guide you. There is a path for everyone to follow. My journey has begun. So, wherever you are in your life, take a moment, step back, take a few deep breaths and appreciate the gift of mindfulness.

Dedicated to my friend Janet.

Mindful Exercise:
Accepting Your Natural Beauty

When you glance into a mirror, who do you see? Someone whose years are passing by?

When you look at yourself in a mirror, don't just glance. I invite you to take the time to look a little closer and investigate who you see.

1. Take a few moments to look at the outer skin of the beautifully strong and unique person that you are.

2. Explore your facial expressions, smile, look at the shape and contours of your features.

3. Bring your awareness down from the top of your head to your forehead, eyebrows, eyes – notice the beauty in your eyes, their colour, your reflection looking back. Notice your nose, chin, cheekbones, jawline, lips; their shape and colour.

4. Bring your hands to gently caress your face. Feel the temperature and softness of your skin.

5. Accept gratitude for your senses: sight, smell, taste, hearing, touch.

Notice how this exercise makes you feel. Journal your thoughts, accepting your natural beauty that time has kindly delivered to you. Repeat this exercise once a week and feel gratitude for your natural beauty.

Guided Meditation: Visualising Nature

Spending time in nature is one of the most enjoyable ways to be mindful. In this guided meditation, I encourage you to explore nature by visualising the colours, sounds and smells you might encounter. I hope you enjoy the journey. Listen to this guided meditation at <u>TeachMindfulnessOnline.com/transform</u>.

About Susan Haigh

Susan is a personal holistic therapist. She loves spending time in nature and appreciates and is grateful for all the universe has to offer.

www.suehaigh.co.uk

14

Finding My Way Back to Mindfulness, One Deep Breath at a Time

~ *Jess Lambert*

Many years ago, a therapist gave me a CD (that's how long ago it was!) with some mindfulness exercises led by Jon Kabat-Zinn. The exercise I really took to was the body scan: thirty minutes of stillness in my body, in my mind, as I listened to his voice, calming me with that soft Bostonian accent. There's a line he says that still gives me goosebumps and often brings tears to my eyes: "As long as you are breathing, there's more right with you than wrong with you." Such a simple reminder. I am breathing, I am alive.

Life isn't linear, it isn't straight, and there are always bumps in the road. My life took me to London and, although I had good intentions to join a mindfulness group, I forgot. I got caught up in London life, as it's so easy to do, and I stopped practising. Work, commuting, marathon training, watching gigs, playing gigs, meeting friends . . . all this became my life, until my body started acting up. I put it down to stress. I was a hospital social worker, covering most of the Central London hospitals. I loved and hated my work in equal measure: loving the stories people would tell, helping people, and the drive and the buzz; yet hating the paperwork, the bureaucracy, and the worry I would make mistakes and disappoint my colleagues, or even find myself part of a social work media story. I continually struggled to reconcile those feelings.

My life changed on a Saturday. A trip to the hospital and a diagnosis later, I was put on medication and within a week I felt as though I'd had the wind knocked out of me. I could barely get out of bed, I felt like I was walking through molasses, and I no longer had any interest in anything other than getting home, curling up on the sofa and watching endless TV. I struggled to work; I struggled to be sociable and friendly; I had no desire to do anything other than sleep.

A couple of months in, while I was battling with a change in medication, a friend introduced me to yoga. She was training to be a yoga teacher, so she came over to my flat and worked through some poses with me and recommended an online platform where I could practise. I randomly discovered another teacher who clicked with me with her playful style, and her clear, deep knowledge of yoga. She taught in Islington, not far from where I lived, so I started attending her classes once a week. Most weeks I couldn't do much, and I often found myself resting in child's pose or crying through Shavasana. She didn't mind though, and she gave me the space in her class to do so.

When she announced she was doing a weekend retreat, I signed up – and I rediscovered mindfulness. A guest teacher. A tiny, bubbly person with flame-red hair and a big smile, she introduced us to mindfulness, to stillness, to settling. She announced she was doing an eight-week course, and I felt inspired to sign up.

We met every week in a tiny little room right in the bustle of the city. I struggled, as I believe many of us do when we start mindfulness. We're so used to doing stuff, rushing about, filling our diaries – we believe that if we're not busy, then we're not being productive. We never stop to observe our bodies and our minds, or try to understand what they might be telling us. It was a slow process for me. I would often forget to practise, and it took a while to figure out the best time for me to instigate mindfulness practice into my day, and then commit to continuing.

I had been a runner for many years, so my breath had always been important. As a runner, you become aware of how you breathe as you run, trying to find that sweet spot of a comfortable rhythm and a steady breath, but I'd never thought about my breath in any other way until I started yoga and mindfulness. I started to see my breath differently; it became more important to me to understand my breath and how it related to the different emotions that would course through my body on any given day. I took time to check in with my breath, and I used it to calm myself. I would do conscious breathing on the way to meetings or assessments, when I was feeling anxious, or when I was starting to flag during the day.

About six months after starting my medication, I decided to take a break from work. I didn't feel I was able to give my all and I still struggled to get up every morning. I moved to Spain to teach English as a foreign language, and while there I completed Shamash Alidina's online course in how to teach mindfulness. I also decided to do my yoga teacher training. It was great. I enjoyed both practices, made them a regular part of my life, and was looking forward to teaching them to others – showing people what I'd learnt and how they too could find a little stillness in their lives. On moving back to the UK, I often incorporated mindfulness into my yoga classes and I received some great feedback.

I'd like to say that life was amazing from then, that I maintained my practice, that I became Zen. Alas, my heart got broken and I slipped. I lost my regular yoga practice, though I would still try and meditate as often as I could, trying to work through my pain and grief. I then got my heart broken again and that was it. I lost both of my practices. Completely. I knew I needed to do them, knew that they would both help me work through the emotions – the pain, anger, loss and grief – but I couldn't. I came to almost fear my yoga mat. I didn't want to sit with my breath because I knew I might cry – and then what?

It's taken me two years to build back my mindfulness practice and to be able to sit with my breath again. Yoga is following, but it's much slower. Yet I am thankful for the practice I had before because, without this, I think I would be floundering even more. What I learnt gave me a solid foundation and understanding of how mindfulness can benefit me every single day. Part of this is understanding that mindfulness doesn't always involve sitting on my meditation cushion and focusing on my breath: it may mean taking time out of my work day to walk and feel the sunshine on my skin, or taking a few moments to enjoy a cup of tea or coffee, or even just to sit and look out of the window. Yet mindfulness is also a part of how we are with other people and how we show up in our lives, such as giving someone your full attention while they talk. This is especially important in a job like social work, a job I've come back to after four and a half years away.

It feels like this is the end of the story, but it isn't, not really. It never really is, is it? People have tapestries of stories – patchwork quilts, perhaps – that cover all their thoughts and experiences, and although each experience shapes us, it's never the end of the story until we draw our final breath. The route of mindfulness is never-ending, and it's not always a smooth journey. The best thing about it, for me, is that there is always scope for change, for adaptation, for learning. Will I maintain this practice every day for the rest of my life? Unlikely. I know I'll slip on some days, and that's okay. Is this practice something I can work on for the rest of my life? You bet it is. Does that bring me hope? Absolutely.

Mindfulness practice isn't easy. If you've lost your way, it's okay; if you're struggling, it's okay. Just remember: it all comes down to the present moment and each breath, which is always there, always accessible and always waiting.

Mindful Exercise:
Noticing Change

This mindful exercise can help you become aware of the ever-changing nature of the world we live in.

1. Wherever you are, take a moment to notice the sky. Is it blue? Is it cloudy? What kind of clouds can you see? Is the sky grey? Is it dark? Can you see the stars?

2. Wherever you are, what can you smell? This might be trees or flowers outside, maybe food or the smell of fresh laundry. Just notice it and take the time to take a deep breath in and then a long, slow breath out. You can simply take one deep breath, or you may wish to do more.

3. Remind yourself that everything is always changing. Look up at the sky at different times during the day and this will become very apparent. Even on the sunniest of days, the colour of the sky will change from morning to afternoon, evening to night.

Use this exercise if things in your life feel beyond your control, if change is happening and it feels overwhelming, or if you simply need a moment in your day to step back from everything and reset.

Guided Meditation: Change Is Always with Us

Change is a constant in our lives, and the way we feel can change from moment to moment. This guided meditation helps you recognise and observe these changes without judgement. Listen to the guided meditation at
TeachMindfulnessOnline.com/transform.

About Jess Lambert

Jess is a social worker in Cambridge, UK. She recently returned to the profession after a career break, which included spending time in Mallorca and Glasgow teaching yoga and English as a foreign language. Jess is a singer-songwriter and has released three EPs, with a debut album coming soon.

15

Learning to Surf:
Accepting Life's Events

~ Elspeth Lewis

"How much time do you think he has left?" I asked the cancer charity volunteer, as we all sat around the small kitchen table of my childhood family home in Belfast.

"Well, let me put it this way," he responded in broad Belfast tones,

"I wouldn't be rushin' out to buy him any Easter eggs, like, you know?"

Easter was four weeks away. Two days after this insightful conversation (one which we now look back on with much humour), Dad died.

I awoke intuitively in the very early hours of 9th March 2015, after a couple of hours' sleep, and went downstairs to find Dad with a Marie Curie night nurse and my sister by his side.

I went to wake my brother and we all sat together around Dad's bed in the living room as he struggled to breathe. His condition was rapidly deteriorating. The pain and effort to breathe was forcing his whole body to writhe and contract. He was really labouring to die, and it made me feel powerless to watch.

Eventually, Dad let go of his struggle and passed away.

Five years earlier, we had been sitting beside Mum's bed – set up next door in our family dining room – as she gradually and quietly slipped away, after more than two years of living with the same terminal cancer as Dad. Hers was a very different, peaceful death. I remember listening to the rhythm of her breathing, as her breaths became further and further apart, and the sounds of the multitude of machinery around her, which continued to whirr and click for some time after she had passed away.

A few days after Dad's death, I returned to Scotland to collect my daughters before going back to Belfast for the funeral. Now an adult orphan, also in the midst of a challenging divorce, I felt exposed, vulnerable and directionless. Even having lived away from home for 17 years, I felt rudderless. If it hadn't been for my children, my life would have seemed pointless and empty.

Work was also demanding and stressful. It felt like there was no respite anywhere in my life. The only chink of light at the time was my children, who kept me functioning. The basic requirements of parenting enabled me to keep putting one foot in front of the other.

However, this in itself was a problem. Without understanding the real importance of self-care at that time, I tried to keep on going and going. I made light of what was happening to me and mostly brushed off other people's concerns. Lots of people went through divorce and bereavement, so surely I could deal with this, too?

One morning, shortly after my dad's funeral, I woke up and couldn't move my body. It was an incredibly frightening sensation and I still struggle to describe it. It was as if everything had shut down. The connection between my mind and my body simply refused to work. All of the events of the last five years had come to a head and my body was saying "no more".

It only lasted thirty seconds at the most, but the shock of the experience jolted me into action. Although my mind was telling me that there was nothing worth getting out of bed for, I pushed myself to get up and move. I fully believe now that this was my transcendent self in action – my ability to take a step back and observe what was taking place. A wider awareness that I could either choose to lie in bed and be miserable, or I could choose to slowly and gently start to move forward.

My GP signed me off work for six weeks, which was the breathing space I needed. I was facing numerous challenges, including clearing a family home in a different country with my siblings; single-parenting two young children; and dealing with bereavement and divorce.

When I returned to work, I felt as if I had lost all my motivation. People assume that just because you're physically back at work, everything is fine again, but healing doesn't magically happen over a six-week period. My mind was constantly scanning for threats around me. I had become so used to overwhelming crises, beyond my control, that my mind had forgotten what 'normal' looked like.

It was nine years between my mum being diagnosed with terminal cancer – in the same week that my first daughter was born – and me finally receiving my hand-delivered divorce papers in the summer of 2016. Nine years of continuous upheaval, and now I had to begin to build a new 'normal'.

Part of building my new normal involved me taking time to learn to breathe properly again. I noticed that I would often hold my breath as my mind got swept away in rumination. I wasn't breathing fully and had been diagnosed with costochondritis (an inflammation of the cartilage between the ribs), alongside several other health issues.

Simply sitting, listening to a meditation app and breathing for a few minutes, was a new experience for me. I had practised hypnobirthing and yoga, but I hadn't taken time to check in with myself much at all since becoming a parent.

To begin with, the opportunity to sit quietly was an escape. Anytime I felt overwhelmed, I did a short mindfulness meditation. I remember thinking: "Wow, this is more effective than a glass of wine!" Meditation felt much more fulfilling!

Eventually, after taking longer courses on the Headspace app, then an eight-week mindfulness-based stress reduction (MBSR) course and establishing a daily meditation practice, I realised that I wanted to share this wonderful life skill with others. I decided to train to teach mindfulness with Shamash Alidina, which was life-changing for me. Teaching mindfulness deepened my own personal practice and allowed me to experience a more fulfilling life through sharing my knowledge with others.

The main transformations I have experienced, thanks to my mindfulness practice, are:

- Connecting: developing meaningful connections with others, and connecting more deeply with nature and the world around me.
- Observing: being able to sit with challenging thoughts and emotions, and allowing space for these experiences to take place and then pass by. (This is the 'transcendent' or 'observer' self, when we aren't deeply entangled in the 'story' of what is happening.)
- Being self-compassionate: being aware of my inner critic and learning to speak more kindly to myself.
- Values-based living: placing more emphasis on leading a values-based, full and meaningful life, which for me means enjoying and learning from the journey, rather than being focused so much on the end goal or destination.

The key lesson that I have taken from bringing mindfulness to my post-traumatic growth is that we have no control over life events. They just happen. Sometimes these events are all-consuming, overwhelming and feel as if they may be never-ending. We can feel like victims and experience a sense of injustice, which causes us to become stuck. When we are willing to accept challenging life events and to respond as best we can, our suffering eases.

Whenever I feel small or helpless now, I am able to show myself compassion. I no longer force myself to keep going when times are challenging. Instead, I allow myself to rest. I have flourished as a result. I have undertaken exciting challenges which I would never have dreamt of before – and I know I have my mindfulness practice to thank for that.

In the words of Jon Kabat-Zinn: *"You can't stop the waves, but you can learn to surf."*

Swimming against the tide is exhausting, and sometimes we need to simply accept how things are and ride the waves.

Mindful Exercise:
SURF

To help you cope with life events, try this short mindful exercise towards acceptance.

S – STEP BACK

Sit, lie down or stand upright. Take a deep breath in and out, as you set an intention to create a warm and welcoming space for whatever might be present in this moment. Become aware of your surroundings, noticing what you can see, hear, touch, smell and taste. Observe with kindness any bodily sensations, thoughts and feelings. You may like to imagine that you are lying on a surfboard, as the waves of thoughts, feelings and sensations rise and fall around you.

U – UNHOOK

Remember that you are not your thoughts and feelings. If you become aware of the presence of unhelpful thoughts or emotions, such as "I'm not good enough," try unhooking from these by saying to yourself, "I notice that I'm having the thought that I'm not good enough," or "I notice that there is anxiety present." As a curious observer, explore this further by noticing where you feel this emotion in your body, and what type of sensation it is producing: is it pulsing, tingling, warm?

R – RIDE THE WAVES

When we become caught up in a struggle with difficult thoughts and feelings, it is often like being pulled under a large wave. Be aware of your thoughts and feelings coming and going in waves, as you breathe in and out. Some waves may seem overwhelming, but they will eventually pass and subside back into the ocean.

F – FREEDOM

Allowing the situation to be as it is enables you to experience a sense of freedom as you move forwards. By cultivating a friendly and caring attitude, you may say words such as, "I notice I'm having a really challenging time right now," and care for yourself in the same way as you would care for a good friend.

You may experience some resistance towards showing yourself warmth and compassion, but by practising SURF, you should notice that the suffering eases.

Guided Meditation: Sea Glass Meditation

This short meditation can help you to cultivate acceptance. By noticing that all beings, matter and energy are constantly changing, you can become more accepting of change in your own life. Listen to the meditation at TeachMindfulnessOnline.com/transform.

About Elspeth Lewis

Elspeth is a mindfulness coach and parent of two girls, based in Edinburgh. Elspeth loves the beach and is passionate about racial justice and ACT (Acceptance and Commitment Training/Therapy). She shares mindfulness with others through her business Pause to Be.

www.pausetobe.co.uk

16

Mindfulness as the Foundation
for a Happy, Healthy Life

~ *Jason Maraschiello*

Mindfulness has always felt like a form of internal martial arts to me. Sometimes its presence is hard to recognise until you metaphorically find yourself in a dark alley faced with a mugger. As they move to attack, you discover that you know kung fu, and you are able to redirect the attack and disarm the assailant. Mindfulness offers a very 'wax-on, wax-off' approach to surviving the trials of life. In the toughest times in my life when I have felt scared, in trouble or lost, my mindfulness practice would come into play – like when the hidden powers of your favourite superhero kick in at the last minute to save the day, showing you what they're truly made of.

I was first introduced to the practice of mindfulness at the age of ten. I went to a book fair and was told I could choose any book I liked. I came across a book about controlling minds and the incredible potential of mental fortitude. As a ten-year-old bullied outcast who was constantly picked on, the thought of controlling people's minds seemed very appealing! As I read, the book took me in an unexpected direction, leading me through different meditation practices and concepts that explained that I didn't have to accept the negative things the bullies said about me as reality. I realised that even if they hurt my body, they couldn't hurt the real me underneath the skin.

However, by the time I was thirteen, I was suffering from adolescent depression and had contemplated taking my own life. We had just moved to a new town, and having no friends and being the punching bag for all my classmates was taking its toll. I remember crying myself to sleep, not understanding why I was even on this planet. It was in that dark time that a knowing came into my mind, seemingly out of nowhere: I just knew that even though life inevitably had pain in it, I could choose how much I let myself suffer from that pain.

I remembered a story I'd read in that old book of mine about 'the second arrow'. The first arrow represents the pain we face in our lives and have little control over; perhaps a break-up, the loss of a loved one, or even something physical like the loss of a limb. The second arrow is the mental turmoil and suffering we put ourselves through as a result of the first arrow. We often allow those thoughts to cause us more damage than the initial pain we experience.

After contemplating suicide, I decided to stay on this earth and make the most out of every moment. I made a pact with myself to explore and experience all that life had to offer. In high school, I went from being a 90-pound asthmatic child with no friends to being Student Council President, Band President, and captain of both the Wrestling Team and the Improv Team. I joined every other club and team I could.

I would always meditate before every match, game or competition, and eventually I started teaching my fellow students how we could use mindfulness and meditation to become focused and centred.

Through college I had an open-door policy to help anyone who felt the stress and anxiety of student life. I wanted to share this gift of a practice I had stumbled upon so many years ago.

As with all things in life, my practice came and went in waves. When I graduated and started working in the corporate world, my practice suffered – I felt the pressure of needing to live my life the way others told me I should. I was working up to 80 hours a week, with little sleep. I felt disconnected from the light that had shone so brightly within me for so many years. The patterns of stress and anxiety started creeping back into my life, and I was on the brink of burnout.

One night, I was lying in bed talking to my girlfriend about how she felt stuck in her job and stifled by the way she was living her life. I started consoling her, telling her, "You are never stuck; you always have the choice to make your reality as you want it to be." I suddenly realised these were the very words I needed to hear for myself. In a moment, the little flicker of light that had been on low for the past years roared back into life within me.

We sold our possessions, got married and decided to travel the world. We spent two years backpacking through seven countries, learning how different people from around the world view life and define success. We learnt from the nomadic Indigenous Australians in northern Arnhem Land, discussed philosophy with Buddhists in Thailand, studied yoga in ashrams in India, and (probably most powerfully of all) simply sat and watched the sun rise over the Himalayas with the mountain tribes in Nepal. I discovered so much about what it truly means to be 'in the moment'.

During our travels, there was a growing calling to return to Canada, where it all started. I knew I could stay in any of those remote places and live out my days studying the ancient practices designed to help people connect with their true nature, but part of me felt as if that would be taking the easy path – running away from my stress instead of learning to work with it.

After two years of travel we decided to head home, trusting that we would know the path to take as it presented itself to us. We built a tiny home on my parents' property and started taking odd jobs to make money. Despite telling ourselves that we wouldn't let the hustle and bustle of the Western world affect us the way it had before, it was easier said than done. We ended up experiencing culture shock. It was difficult to see so much wasted food and resources, and observe the overwhelming consumer mentality: we were disturbed by the fresh realisation that relentless marketing makes us feel dissatisfied unless we buy the newest and shiniest things.

We decided to do our best to help people see that they have everything they need to be happy within them at any given moment. My wife started teaching yoga, and I started offering free lectures and workshops on mindfulness and meditation. We eventually opened our own mindfulness and yoga centre. After further training, I started doing sessions with people suffering from post-traumatic stress disorder, anxiety and depression. Coming full circle from my own dark days, I also offered suicide intervention and support.

Life has a way of testing us and reminding us that mindfulness is like a muscle: if we stop practising, it becomes weaker. A couple of years ago, all in the span of six months, I lost my grandmother and my aunt, my marriage went through rocky times, my father needed quadruple heart bypass surgery, my mother had issues with her liver, and my best friend's fiancée committed suicide. I was again humbled and brought back to the same simple meditations I had discovered in that first book on mind control. I had become caught up in the role of teacher and forgot to, first and foremost, always remain a student to the lessons life has to teach.

Life can be painful, but if we pause to appreciate the little gifts we are given in the smallest moments then it can be so much more. Pure joy or bliss can live in the smile of a stranger or in a scent carried on a warm breeze. When I think how mindfulness transformed my life, I am simply reminded to smile. Mindfulness didn't so much change my life as become the foundation for my life. It is the safety net that I can always rely on to catch me if I fall, and knowing it is there allows me to soar to whatever heights I can imagine without fear.

Many ancient philosophies suggest that life isn't meant to be easy – that it is the discomfort that brings the lessons, the lessons that bring the growth, and the growth that makes life worth living.

Mindful Exercise:
Becoming the Observer

As we navigate our way through life, it is important to continue to exercise our minds so that they are strong enough to handle the lessons life sends our way. This exercise helps us to strengthen the part of the brain that allows us to choose how we respond to everyday situations.

1. Find a place with few distractions and get into a comfortable position.
2. Begin to think of things like mosquitoes, lice, fleas, spiders: all that is itchy, scratchy and squirmy.
3. Eventually, you will feel an itch develop somewhere on your body. Do not scratch it at first.
4. Observe where you are itchy: notice how it feels, notice the stories your mind creates about it and, most importantly, notice that you have the willpower not to scratch it.
5. After observing, even for just a few seconds, you can now choose to scratch the itch.

Try practising this regularly, including on occasions when an itch arrives naturally. Eventually, you will train your mind to respond to a situation instead of reacting to one. You are telling your brain that you want to have a conscious say in how you handle situations in your life. This little exercise can be the starting point to choosing how you handle confrontation, fear, anxiety and stress.

Guided Meditation: Spotlight Meditation

We are often our greatest critics through life, which holds us back from fully stepping into our greatness. In this meditation you will be visualising yourself on a grand stage, stepping into the spotlight and recognising how much you really have to offer the world and the community around you. Listen to this meditation at TeachMindfulnessOnline.com/transform.

About Jason Maraschiello

Jason runs retreats, workshops, talks and training all around the world, virtually and in person, focusing on mindfulness and mental health. He owns a yoga studio and wellness centre in Canada and strives to create a community that is focused on bringing positivity to people's lives.

www.HigherPotentialLiving.com

17

Letting Go of the Past and Embracing the Present

~ *Yvonne Cookson*

For many years, my life was extremely tough. My earliest memories of feeling anxious and sad were around aged ten. I felt immense fear, dread and worry. Simple decisions became unnerving and daunting. Often my mind would spiral out of control with fearful thoughts. As time went on, I found it harder and harder to get off the rollercoaster. These experiences carried on into my adult life.

Stress and anxiety regularly filled my days and nights. I didn't sleep well; it would take me hours to fall asleep, and I would wake early with my mind already racing before I'd even had time to open my eyes and catch my breath. My diet was extremely poor, too; I either didn't eat or I binged, which resulted in my weight fluctuating. I was consumed by feelings of guilt.

I regularly lived in the distant past, allowing myself to feel like a victim, and my worries about the future caused me immense anxiety.

I turned to prescription drugs. I tried a multitude of different medications – some helped, some made me feel ten times worse. But I knew drugs weren't the answer; they were just a short-term fix.

Having children changed everything for me. I had two little people I had to be responsible for, so I began to try and heal myself and improve my life. I realised I had a purpose: to become the best version of myself I could be, and to hold onto my belief that there was a better way for me to live.

I opened my world to a variety of practices and holistic treatments. I went to weekly counselling sessions; I tried reiki (and became a reiki master myself); I worked with crystals and discovered crystal healing; I attended sound bath therapy sessions; I tried various massage treatments; and I created vision boards. I turned to psychic healers and became involved in shamanic rituals and treatments. These therapeutic practices definitely made me feel better and I became more positive in the short term, but, in reality, it was like sticking a plaster over a deep cut that never fully healed.

No matter how hard I tried, I still didn't feel fully in control. I existed for my girls, trying to consistently show them a brave face. I dreaded going in to work – always concealing how I actually felt and pretending to be the strong and happy extrovert, when all I wanted to do was curl into a ball and be left alone. Friendships and relationships became strained, as I couldn't let anyone past the barrier I had built up over the years. Even holidays weren't enjoyable, as the whole time I was meant to be enjoying myself, I couldn't stop thinking about going back to real life.

Everything felt like an uphill struggle. However, I never lost hope and I knew there had to be something else, something more effective that would enable me to live the life I knew I deserved.

Thankfully, I found mindfulness. I honestly cannot believe how much it has transformed me and my mindset. When I started learning how to practise mindfulness, it seemed extremely alien to me, but early into an eight-week course I began to feel intense changes happening within me and altering the way I thought.

Mindfulness has enabled me to change my mindset from being stressed, scared and anxious to welcoming gratitude, positivity and acceptance. I am now able to distance myself from my thoughts, and I no longer find my mind in a constant turmoil of questions, challenges and worries. I live from moment to moment, which helps me to focus on what's happening right now rather than on what has happened in the past or what might occur in the future.

Admittedly, not every day is easy, and mindfulness is certainly not a cure-all, but I am so much stronger and more resilient than before. Meditation keeps me in tune with my mind and my body, which enables me to notice changes or anything unusual. I am able to bring myself back to the present moment in most situations and move forward without holding on to any baggage. If I have a stressful moment, I know how to stop it from getting out of control by simply using my breath.

Mindfulness has been a game changer for me in every way. It has become a way of living and thinking. I now wake up most days feeling refreshed, with a clear mind, and I always spend a few mindful minutes in bed before I get up: practising gratitude and being present; noticing how my body feels, my breath, and any sounds around me. Starting my day in such a positive way is extremely powerful – it helps me feel calmer and stronger so I can carry on in a mindful and assured way.

People often say that they don't have time to be mindful, but I believe it's a way of living that can be infused into pretty much everything in life. I notice more of the world around me when I'm out walking: the different colours of the leaves on the trees, the sounds of the birds singing, and the smell of flowers and cut grass. I am always fully present when talking to my partner, a friend or a colleague. I cook in a mindful way by noticing the smells, flavours and textures, and I even brush my teeth mindfully. Most of these things started to happen without me even noticing: although my practice started with a couple of very basic techniques, mindfulness naturally found its way into different aspects of my life. I don't have to think about being mindful, because it just happens.

So, do I think mindfulness can change your life? I can honestly say, hand on heart, that yes – it most definitely can. It has saved me from a life of unhappiness, stress and anxiety. It has changed who I am, who I am becoming and how I think. My connection and relationship with both of my beautiful daughters is fantastic: healthy and well-balanced. After many years of bad relationships, I have found the love of my life and have an incredibly loving and sincere relationship. I have let go of my past and all that was in it. I live for now and I don't worry about what may be around the corner.

Mindfulness opened up a way to an easier, happier life and changed everything for me, and all I did was welcome it with open arms and embrace the way it made me feel.

I hope that sharing my journey has helped you in some way.

Mindful Exercise:
Mindful Gratitude Reminder

Gratitude and mindfulness work hand in hand. When I first started to practise gratitude, I used the following exercise to remind myself regularly to be grateful; now it comes naturally to me throughout my day.

Gratitude grows – the more you feel thankful for, the more you find yourself noticing new things to be grateful for.

1. Choose a small rock or crystal – make sure it's one you like because of its shape, colour or texture, or because it is special to you.

2. Put the rock/crystal in a place where you will see or feel it throughout your day, such as in your pocket or on your desk. Every time you feel it or look at it, think of one thing you are grateful for.

3. When you take the rock/crystal out of your pocket or off your desk at the end of the day, take a few minutes to think about all the things you've been grateful for that day.

Repeat this process daily and see how amazing you feel after a very short period of time.

Guided Meditation: Gratitude Meditation

True gratitude is good for you and your relationships. Science suggests that practising gratitude aids your health, as well as expanding your happiness. This gratitude meditation helps you to connect to the things you feel grateful for in your life. Listen to the meditation at TeachMindfulnessOnline.com/transform.

About Yvonne Cookson

Yvonne is a mindfulness teacher and holistic therapist. Mindfulness has changed her life, and now she wants to help change the lives of others for the better.

www.serenitawellness.co.uk

18

Mindfulness Is a Journey, Self-compassion Is Its Outcome

~ Nahid Dave

After a lot of calming self-affirmations, I started the first day of my third year at medical school after summer break. It wasn't going to be like any other day.

"Everyone is going to ask me why my face looks different. I will have to explain to my best friend why I didn't tell her earlier. She will be able to help me; some people may ask her instead of directly asking me."

I was born with a cleft lip and at the onset of my teenage years I had concluded that I looked unattractive. I was very aware of my defects, and conscious of my looks. Over that summer, I had undergone surgery to raise the nasal bridge, lighten the scar and straighten the border of my upper lip. Today was the day I thought I would face questions about my face and find a way to live in my 'new normal'.

My apprehension was palpable: my hands were cold and clammy, and I had to calm my racing thoughts as I entered college. A sea of familiar faces, smiles and hugs flooded the hallway. We settled in for the classes; my best friend sat next to me, but she didn't mention anything.

I thought to myself, "I have lived 17 years of my life with a puckered upper lip, a scar below my nose and a flattened nose. Has no one even noticed it?"

After class I asked my friend, "Do you notice anything different about my appearance?"

She studied me carefully and said, "Oh yes! I was about to ask you." I felt a sense of relief and prepared to answer all the questions I had rehearsed responses to throughout the holidays. Instead, she said, "I like your new haircut, it really suits you."

I was bewildered and lost for words. I didn't explain myself, but I couldn't sleep that night. I needed answers.

"Was I so irrelevant that no one stopped to notice? Had I created an illusion of being 'ugly' – was this only in my head? Did I not become prettier with corrective surgery – or maybe I wasn't ugly the whole time?"

I didn't get any answers that night; I had to wait a few years before I found them.

My first encounter with mindfulness occurred a few years later, when I discovered a quote by Jon Kabat-Zinn: "It's not a matter of letting go – you would if you could. Instead of 'let it go' we should probably say 'let it be'."

I thought I understood the words, but didn't know how this understanding could translate into real life. Intrigued, I signed up for a three-day mindfulness retreat, praying I would last through the silent meditation practice. It was my first time trying meditation; I was worried that I wouldn't be able to sit still. I didn't realise that this was going to be the first day of a life-changing experience.

We were seated on the floor in a traditional Indian setting; there was calmness in the silence, with the occasional sound of a Tibetan singing bowl. The ambience created an atmosphere of safety, even though I was in a room full of strangers.

After an introduction to mindfulness, its roots, and its attitudinal foundations, we began a sitting meditation. I found it difficult to just 'be' and not have anything to do. I couldn't remember ever doing that. For the first few minutes, my thoughts drifted to the journey I had taken to reach the retreat. I noticed I could smell lavender in the room. I lost track of time as my thoughts moved through different parts of my life. I returned again to the first day I entered medical school after surgery; I thought about the times I would stay burrowed in my phone because I was self-conscious of my looks in public; and I remembered my sister's wedding when I couldn't fit into my dress.

The residue of these thoughts and sensations resurfaced, and I found my cheeks wet as the tears rolled down. I had boxed away these incidents, so I could pretend they didn't exist – but now they had found me again.

We were asked to spend some time reflecting on our experience. As everyone began to open up and share, there was an energy binding all the participants together.

I had just experienced 'impermanence' – that things will always change, like a river flowing past different pebbles over time. I didn't consciously drive my mind to focus on something or distract myself from the unpleasant memories; the thoughts didn't stop, but instead kept changing effortlessly.

The retreat's instructor asked us to merely observe our thoughts and not argue with them, react to them or push them aside. We were 'being' with our thoughts rather than 'doing' something with them.

After the first practice, I couldn't wait to learn more about mindfulness and my mind and body. We were guided to be attentive, noticing different sensations in the body, which helped us form a better connection with our minds through self-realisation. I realised that meditation isn't about clearing the mind of all thoughts after all.

For the rest of the retreat, we tried different meditations, including the body scan, eating and walking meditations, followed by periods of reflection and sharing our experiences. As I explored my bodily sensations, I discovered my self-esteem, my anger, my pain, and feelings of love and bliss.

I experienced the difference between knowledge and wisdom. In medical school, I'd learnt about the anatomy and physiology of the human body – that was knowledge. Through mindfulness, I experienced how the mind and body truly connect – that developed wisdom. Mindfulness gives us the freedom to seek answers, but it doesn't provide them. The open-ended nature of mindfulness appealed to me.

The retreat was my first step into mindfulness. Afterwards, I started reading books by Jon Kabat-Zinn and Mark Epstein, and I attended a few more meditation programmes. I also began to practise mindfulness every day.

Years later, even though I was not striving to find the answers any more ('non-striving' being a pillar of mindfulness practice), I found some answers to the questions that had eluded me since the first day of medical school after my surgery.

I met a client who had a cleft lip. She was self-conscious and had low self-esteem. She told me about her struggles, and I thought to myself, "I have made peace with this, and I am now in a comfortable place. I can help someone who has similar demons."

I thought I would be able to maintain my objectivity so that I could help her, and yet every now and again I felt a slight tug and found myself reliving some of my own memories. I then became aware that I was being mindless, so I invited my mind to be in the present and to be compassionate towards myself.

That's when it occurred to me: "Mindfulness is a path that helps me feel compassion towards myself. It is not a destination but a journey, and I will continue to have new insights for the rest of my life."

I started training in mindfulness as a lifestyle and also as a form of therapy. As I evolve and grow, so do my patients. When people talk to me about low self-esteem, and when the concept of self-compassion seems alien to them, I know what they mean. It's not easy to be non-judgemental towards ourselves: we live in a world of standardisation and comparison.

I am complete just the way I am. There is nothing I can dislike about myself. Compassion begins with loving myself. I saw the world through a filter; a prejudiced opinion about beauty and self. I was never ugly: no one ever is. I was and am complete.

Mindful Exercise:
Self-acceptance

A sense of acceptance and awareness towards your emotions and experiences has the power to ease suffering. You may find it helpful to try this exercise once a week, to check in with yourself and see if there are any pent-up emotions or worries that you have been avoiding.

1. Sit in an undisturbed place and close your eyes. Focus on the normal rhythm of your breath.

2. Think of an incident, image or experience that made you feel a negative emotion.

3. Notice the sensations in your body as you relive it. Be aware of the thoughts and the emerging emotions.

4. If you feel that you are suffering, accept it. The desire to be free from suffering is suffering in itself. As a human being, you will experience a full range of emotions. Accept all your emotions and thoughts. Tell yourself: "I am not my thoughts."

5. Hold both your hands together, like a handshake. As you breathe, notice the warmth pass through your hands, as you feel care and acceptance towards yourself. Tell yourself: "I am there for me. And I am enough."

When you complete the exercise, you may feel a sense of relief, completeness and oneness.

Guided Meditation: Self-compassion Meditation

Compassion towards others may come easily to you. We are able to look beyond the flaws of others. However, self-compassion, while equally important, is often a neglected aspect of our being. This guided meditation takes you through showing yourself compassion, as you would show compassion to anyone else who was suffering. Listen to the guided meditation at TeachMindfulnessOnline.com/transform.

About Nahid Dave

Nahid is a psychiatrist by profession and has been practising in Mumbai, India, for the past six years. She has trained in cognitive behavioural therapy (CBT), rational emotive behaviour therapy (REBT), mindfulness-based stress reduction (MBSR) and teaching mindfulness. She is fond of travelling and writing poems.

www.thoughtmatters.info

19

Mindfulness for a Transformative Recovery

~ Alex Bannard

"We have these places," my German psychotherapist was explaining in her wonderful, sweet-sounding voice, "where a mother can go with her child and just relax, get better."

I began dreaming of a retreat, nice organic food, daily yoga . . . oh, that sounded heavenly. I could even take Indie with me as she was just a toddler.

But the more she talked, the realisation hit home: this wasn't a retreat, this was rehab.

"I'm not famous enough for rehab!" I blurted, and I buried any dreams of going on a retreat and getting better.

This was October 2012: my daughter was 18 months old, my son was four, and I had been diagnosed with severe agitated depression. Life was awful; I was losing it all the time, a raving, screaming banshee. It was toxic and damaging for my kids and my marriage, and I was desperate to fix it – and slightly relieved there was actually something wrong with me that could be fixed, because I was beginning to think it was just me.

And so began several months of trying to work out what support would be available to me, since we were living in Bavaria in Germany for my husband's job and my German was, well, scheisse. I even toyed with the idea of coming back to the UK and checking in to The Priory, but I came to the conclusion that I was definitely not famous enough for that.

Around the same time, I also lost 10kg in weight pretty much overnight. This sudden weight drop alarmed me, since I have problematic lungs: I feared this could signify something more sinister. When I was seven, my dad died, and soon afterwards I came down with a disease that damaged my left lung. This left me prone to chest infections and pneumonia. (I discovered decades later that grief manifests in our lungs, which explains a lot.) Fearing the worst, I got my lungs checked out. I was advised they were no worse than normal, but I begged my doctor: "I know it's extreme, but I would really like to have the affected part of my lung removed. I'm a young mum and I spend every other week in the winter at the doctor's getting antibiotics. This is no life for me or my kids." Being a young mum herself, she got it – so she referred me to a specialist.

The pulmonary specialist's opinion was that if I didn't have the surgery, within ten years my lung would cease to function, which made surgery a no-brainer. It was just a matter of deciding which to treat first: my lung or my mental health.

In the end, I had a quarter of my lung removed in January 2013, and a month later I was admitted to a mental health facility in

Bamberg, around 45 minutes away from home. And this was where my journey to mindfulness really began.

In all honesty, that time was a bit of a blur. I was terribly unwell, and it was traumatic for me to go into hospital for mental health treatment, especially in a foreign country with a language I still struggled with. In the end, I was there for five weeks; when I finally returned home, I was a few steps into the long journey of recovery. My journey started with one step forwards, two steps backwards, but eventually shifted to two steps forwards, one step backwards. My mental health began to improve and I started to feel calmer, safer and happier.

Mindfulness was a huge part of this recovery. I started meditating at Bamberg, but in a self-taught way. One day I did a meditation to connect to my Guardian Angel. The voice guiding the meditation said: "You will receive a message from your Guardian Angel, letting you know they are here for you." Just then my phone buzzed and jarred me out of my meditation. It was a message from my husband! "You are NOT my Guardian Angel – my nemesis, maybe," I thought judgementally, returning to my practice. Years of practice later and my phone is always on silent mode when I'm practising, and I'm nowhere near as judgemental. (My husband is now my ex, but that's a story for another time. Mindfulness is many beautiful and amazing things, but I can't promise it will save a flawed relationship.)

I began practising gratitude on a daily basis, writing down three things I was grateful for – a practice I still maintain to this day. Daily walks in nature were also crucial to my recovery, tapping into the wonderful restorative powers of Mother Nature. I still get out every day, leaving my phone at home, and it's often just me, the dogs and the countryside.

A year and a half after my treatment in Bamberg, we moved to Bangkok for my husband's job. I met a wonderful French lady, Violainne, a practising Buddhist who ran meditation courses. I was in my element and embarked on several courses with her to learn to meditate in the style of the Dalai Lama's school of Buddhism. It was a wonderful way to build on the foundation I had established in my own self-taught practice.

The Buddhist style of meditation is quite prescriptive; it is partially designed to help you receive insights and move towards enlightenment. You have to sit in a certain way, your eyes at a certain angle, just so. I believe you will get more out of a meditation if you are comfortable, but it was a wonderful experience to learn how to meditate 'properly'. Now, I realise there is no such thing a 'proper' meditation. Any meditation is beneficial, even if it's not quite what you were expecting.

Violainne's courses taught me many things: I learnt about metta meditations and loving kindness; I discovered that our thoughts are not facts (wow, what a relief it was to discover that!); and I understood more about compassion and kindness. But Violainne's comment, "It is a work, Alex, it is always a work!" is probably the teaching that resonated most, and I find myself returning to her wise words often.

My mindfulness practice has evolved over the years. It took me from the depths of mental and physical illness and guided me through my recovery. I believe it is when we are most broken that we can find new coping mechanisms and transform. It certainly worked out that way for me.

Meditation is still a daily practice that gives me a few moments of peace, calm and serenity, which helps me to navigate the rest of the day. I also practice and teach yoga, which is a form of mindful movement. I credit both of these practices, together with embracing gratitude and returning to nature daily, as the cornerstones of my recovery and ongoing wellbeing.

But there are other benefits from practising mindfulness. I try to be more accepting, to let go of things that don't serve me or that I cannot change. I am much kinder and more compassionate to myself than I used to be. In those moments when my critical inner voice gets noisy, I remind myself that I wouldn't say that to a friend, so I shouldn't say it to myself – this has been a game changer. I also catch myself when I'm being Little Miss Judgey-pants and try to be less critical. And what's the first step to nipping this judging in the bud? Of course: don't judge the judging!

I'm not perfect, and I still fall from grace, get it wrong, beat myself up occasionally – I'm human, just as we all are. Mindfulness and yoga, or any spiritual practices, don't make you immune from these human frailties, but they do help you to become more aware when you are falling down that rabbit hole. They give you an opportunity to return to yourself more quickly and effectively: to centre, ground and balance yourself.

Ultimately though, it's not a journey to discover mindfulness – mindfulness is the journey. It's not a destination – it's a way of life, a way of being. Mindfulness helped me create a way of living and being that has transformed my life. Whatever inspires you to embrace a mindfulness practice, I believe it will transform your way of living and being too. But it is a work, it is always a work. Maybe that's the point?

Mindful Exercise:
Peace Begins with Me

I was first introduced to this kundalini yoga practice by Gabby Bernstein. It helps you to reconnect to a place of peace and happiness and to centre and ground yourself when you become triggered, anxious, overwhelmed, frustrated, angry – whatever big emotion arises. It only takes a minute or so.

It involves saying a *mantra* (a sound or phrase you can repeat that creates a vibration, which helps to shift you into a place of peace), while you make different accompanying *mudras* (hand gestures). The mantra is: 'peace begins with me'.

Say the mantra with the following mudras:

1. Place your thumb and the tip of your forefinger together (this mudra unites the body with the universe and channels wisdom) and say: **Peace.**
2. Place your thumb and middle finger together (this mudra represents patience) and say: **Begins.**
3. Place your thumb and ring finger together (this mudra helps to generate vitality) and say: **With.**
4. Place your thumb and little finger together (this mudra helps to create clear communication) and say: **Me.**

You can do this practice anywhere, saying the words in your head if you are in public and touching your thumb and fingertips together with each word. I believe this practice helps us to be the change we want to see in the world; after all, if we wish to see peace in challenging times, surely that peace begins with ourselves?

Guided Meditation: Yoga Nidra Body Scan

Yoga nidra is a form of meditation that fosters a sense of deep conscious relaxation. It is typically practised lying down. This meditation brings together visualisation with the body scan: you imagine placing golden stars on each part of your body, directing attention to that area and then allowing the golden healing light to melt into your body. Listen to the guided meditation at TeachMindfulnessOnline.com/transform.

About Alex Bannard

Alex is a qualified yoga and mindfulness teacher living near the Cotswolds in the UK. She offers group sessions, one-to-one and online courses and coaching to clients, helping them to create their own self-care rituals, practices and bliss based around yoga, mindfulness, meditation, nature and gratitude.

www.myananda.co.uk

Part III:

Connecting to Family, Community and the Wider World through Mindfulness

20

The Gentle Power of Mindfulness in Challenging Times

~ *Jacqueline Gammon*

When I'm travelling on an aeroplane, I enjoy sitting by the window and peacefully watching the islands of clouds below. The bump on landing always surprises me, as does the way that my body wants to keep moving forward as the plane slows down. It's a moment that reinforces how fast I have been hurtling through the sky. After the landing comes the inevitable tiredness and slight disorientation of being in a new place as I gather up my bags, disembark and look for signs to point me in the right direction.

I felt the same disorientation when I gave up teaching four years ago. Little did I know that mindfulness would soon set me on the right path.

I had been teaching for over twenty years, fifteen of those in Spain, and I was tired. This was a combination of particularly demanding year groups and trying to support my own children through exams and university. I had little energy for anything other than slumping on the sofa in the evenings. It was not how I wanted to spend the rest of my life. I felt disconnected from myself; I needed a change.

My youngest child would soon be leaving for university in the UK, so it seemed the perfect time to make a change. After much deliberation, I handed in my notice. It was a tough decision after so many years.

I can still see myself at the end of the school year, walking away with a bag of gifts and my now redundant playground whistle. Then came the jolt of realisation that I wouldn't be going back to teaching in September. I loaded up my car and asked myself the overarching question, "What am I going to do next?"

Land. Gather your baggage. Disembark. Look for the signs.

That evening, with perfect synchronicity, I spotted and enrolled on an eight-week mindfulness-based stress reduction (MBSR) course in Barcelona, due to begin in October. I couldn't believe the timing. My sister, a mental health nurse, had introduced me to *The Power of Now* by Eckhart Tolle some time ago, and I was eager to discover more about mindfulness. I had been unsuccessfully looking for a course for a while: now one had appeared as if by magic. I thought it could be the reset button I needed.

Summer passed, September arrived. I packed up my daughter's belongings and travelled to the UK to leave her in her halls of residence, returning home to an empty nest. Everything was different. My fifteen-year routine had stopped. The house was quiet. Suddenly I had more time and less washing.

I spent each day writing. At night, I dreamt that I was late for work.

September turned to October. I found myself lying on a yoga mat in a blissfully scented and darkened room, with what turned out to be several other ex-teachers. We were being guided through a body scan meditation, focusing our awareness on each body part in turn. Someone fell asleep and snored loudly. Others were restless. I listened to the teacher's voice and became aware of the tension that I was holding in my body, particularly in my shoulders, which seemed to have migrated to my ears. My mind was jumping from place to place like a chimp, and it was just as noisy as it tried to disturb my tranquillity. "You're not doing this right!" it screeched. "What are you doing here, anyway?" And, inevitably: "Don't forget to pick up some bread on the way home!"

At the end, we shared our experiences. The teacher kindly told us that there is no right or wrong way to meditate. "Every experience is valid," she said. "It's being able to observe this experience that is important. And whatever thoughts or emotions arise – that's okay, just notice them. Go with the flow. There's no judgement or questions."

Permission to go with the flow. I thought about her words that evening. It was a shock to suddenly realise that I had spent years going against the flow, struggling upstream against my emotions. I would tell myself, "I'm fine. I'm strong. I can juggle and control everything in my life – no problem. Middle age? No problem. Kids moving out? No problem. Stressed out in the classroom? Nah, I've got this, I am a strong woman." These were the stories that I had been telling myself, the same stories that many others tell themselves every day.

It became clear that it was okay to feel what I felt. It was okay to think the thoughts I had, without judgement. It was okay to just be. It was okay to be me. Suddenly I felt lighter.

Land. Gather your bags. Disembark. Look for the signs. Unpack your baggage.

The weeks passed. We learnt about stress and the harm it can do to our bodies and minds when we live in a constant state of fight or flight. I wondered how much damage I'd done to my body over the years with the steady stream of cortisol that must have been pumping through it.

We learnt how to use our breath to calm ourselves and to gauge our stress. It was something I had never thought of before. As I became aware of and connected with my breathing, I wished that I had known about mindfulness years ago – it would have been invaluable in the classroom for dealing with difficult moments.

There were no hours of sitting cross-legged, chanting. 1 quickly came to understand that mindfulness isn't a secret technique: it's a way of life – one that would provide me with resilience in dark times. Above all, it meant better connections, with myself and others.

By the time the course ended, I was meditating regularly at home, putting into practice the tips for mindful living and beginning to see things from a different perspective. I felt more resilient. This was easy! Little did I know that I was about to give mindfulness its first tough test.

On the day of my 49th birthday, my mother was diagnosed with breast cancer. My mind immediately fast-tracked to the future: what was going to happen, would she survive? In my imagination I saw the funeral, the relatives, her empty house and the void in my life. I used my breath to ground myself in the present moment and get back on track. I drew on everything I had learnt in the course, and I meditated.

My sister flew over from England, and we resolved to mindfully focus on each day. Painting a dark picture of the unknown was not going to help anyone, least of all our mother, who needed us to be a calming reference point. We could give her the gift of mindfulness via a ripple effect.

So, in the times when my mother was undergoing tests and we had to wait, we made our way outside into the warm spring sunshine and chatted on a bench. One lunchtime, we ordered nachos in a nearby restaurant and laughed when the waitress brought us each a plate the size of a sombrero. We made the most of this unexpected time together.

The tensest day was the day of the operation. This time we didn't move from the waiting room. We were both quiet, each alone with our thoughts. I didn't touch the book I had brought with me. Mindful breathing stopped me from panicking.

The surgeon came to find us to tell us that the operation had gone well. It was like a moment in a film. The long recovery could now begin.

Weeks later, my sister was back in England and we were chatting on the phone. We both admitted that we wouldn't have coped as well without mindfulness. "I've decided to teach mindfulness!" I announced. "I want to share it with as many people as possible!" I had no idea how I would be able to achieve this as I was living in Spain. Then, with perfect synchronicity, as always, along came an online mindfulness teacher training course (with Shamash Alidina). It was a great match for me. I enjoyed the humour, the supportive community, and the encouragement and confidence to teach mindfulness in a creative, flexible way. Mindfulness has been a welcome gift, but being able to share it with others and hear how their lives have changed is the greatest gift of all.

Mindfulness has a gentle power: the power to gradually change our lives. It helped me to shed years of stress and reconnect with who I am. I've benefited from it through difficult times and will do so again with those yet to come. It has given me an appreciation of the little moments in life, the ones that are often overlooked.

Land. Gather your baggage. Disembark. Look for the signs. Unpack. Enjoy your life – mindfully.

Mindful Exercise:
Letting Go of Your Worries

Worries can often overwhelm us and we become stuck in a cycle of rumination. This exercise is helpful for placing those worries in perspective and releasing them, bringing you calm.

1. Find a quiet moment and write down your worries on small pieces of paper.
2. Spread them out in front of you. Pick one up and read it. Notice your reaction, without judgement.
3. Close your eyes for a moment and take a calming breath, allowing the air to fill your abdomen. Exhale. Open your eyes and place the paper face down.
4. Choose another and repeat the process.
5. When all the pieces are face down, gather them up without re-reading them, shred them and throw them away. Notice how you feel.

I hope this exercise gives you a sense of calm that you can carry into the rest of your day.

Guided Meditation: A Journey to Calm

This guided meditation aims to lead you from overwhelm to calm and relaxation. Listen to the meditation at TeachMindfulnessOnline.com/transform.

About Jacqueline Gammon

Jacqueline is a certified mindfulness teacher, inspiring others to live mindfully in person, online and through her writing. She is based in Spain.

www.gotomindfulness.com

21

Widening Your Perspective
through Mindfulness

~ *Magdalena Živković*

*I am lying on the floor, doing a body scan meditation. Questions
are rushing through my head: "What am I doing? What is this
for? Am I just a silly retired psychologist doing odd things? But if
all these clever people are saying this is something valuable, then
it must be!"*

In 2009, I was 53 and retiring after 29 years of working as a
psychologist in the prison system. I lived with my husband and
his elderly parents, who were in our care. Our grown-up sons were
away, studying and working.

I felt imprisoned by caregiving, somehow contaminated with
sickness, pain and the dullness of my daily routine. My asthma
had deteriorated, so I had to take extra medicine. I took every
spare moment to search the internet for something interesting,
hopeful and meaningful. I read about stress management,
overcoming depression, good nutrition and exercise; I looked for
advice on how to be healthy and happy – but nothing I found

worked. The more I tried to do my best to feel good, the more I sank and ended up feeling worse.

I didn't know if I was depressed or just stressed. I wondered what difference it would make to name it.

Then, in my pursuit of meaning, I came across the book *Full Catastrophe Living* by Jon Kabat-Zinn. Reading it made me feel as if a friend was talking to me. I started to search more about the concept of mindfulness the author wrote about. I took an online mindfulness course. I completed a mindfulness-based stress reduction (MBSR) course. I read more books, including *Mindfulness for Beginners*, also by Jon Kabat-Zinn, *Mindfulness For Dummies* by Shamash Alidina, and *Mindsight* by Daniel J Siegel – and I practised, practised, practised.

It is evening. I am feeding my mother-in-law, who is hardly capable of swallowing. It is taking so long. I am tired, stuck in some dark place, and the same questions are running through my head: "What is the point of all this? Why is all this happening?" And then, from somewhere inside me, came a new idea. "What if I could really feel compassion for her, for her pain, for her being so dependent on me? Not feel sorry for her or pity her, but really be compassionate. How would I feel if I felt only compassion?" I didn't feel it at that moment, but I saw clearly how I might feel differently. It was as if I could see a window somewhere high up, out of reach. It was there, and I believed that looking through that window would really make a difference.

When we were caring for my husband's parents, I didn't know how to befriend pain – to be self-compassionate and allow compassion towards others to unfold from that. It was incredibly transformative when I started to learn how to self-compassionately acknowledge and accept my own experience, no matter how painful it was. I felt a sense of liberation and peace deep in my body. Sometimes it was just for a brief moment, but it was there.

Life went on. My in-laws died. I was occasionally engaged by different organisations as a psychologist, and I progressively incorporated more mindfulness into my work. Privately, I had another huge task. My husband and I had now begun to care for my sick younger sister and my own parents. The situation was equally demanding and painful, but I felt much better this time because I was much more present, much more with my family rather than caught up in my thoughts.

I am spending many hours with my sister. While I am with her, I am only with her. I am not thinking of mindfulness, I am not doing breathing practices, I am not thinking about what to say, I am not thinking about how hard it is, I am not even feeling pain. I am doing simple things for her and leading small, simple conversations about nothing and anything; I am just sitting there when she is silent or asleep. These moments are precious for me and hopefully for her too.

During my sister's last days, I discovered another huge transformational learning experience – I realised how to be present with what I am and what the situation is.

My sister died in 2014. While waiting for the funeral, I started my mindfulness teacher training with Teach Mindfulness Online. In the midst of my own pain, as well as caring for my parents and their pain, I was able to study, learn and create my own teaching programme.

I am sitting with my mother, waiting for a doctor. I am becoming impatient, and I feel very tense. I wonder, "How long is this going to take?" and immediately recognise an uncomfortable feeling in my stomach. "So long!" And then another thought occurs. "Wait, wait! Am I cold? No. Am I hungry? No. Thirsty? No. Am I missing something important? No. So, where is this dissatisfaction coming from? Is it only from the idea that this wait is too long? Can't I just rest in this moment, knowing that I am okay?" I realise that impatience comes from an automatic thought that waiting is uncomfortable. It has nothing to do with the actual experience. "Oh, I need to just get out of my own way. Don't believe everything I think!" The rest of the waiting time I am just breathing and being with my mother. Thoughts may or may not come. If they do, I just go back to my breath. Waiting time becomes mindfulness time.

Another huge transformational insight for me came when I realised that I could intentionally step out of the content of my thoughts as many times as I needed to.

My parents died in 2015 and 2016. I was learning to teach mindfulness during that very hard period of my life. In my teacher training journal, I noted that I would like to teach mindfulness in my community and, today, that is what I do.

In the Croatian language, the expression 'uzeti predah' means 'take a break'. The word 'predah' has within it the word for 'breath' ('dah'), so we literally say, 'take a breath'. I teach people how to drop into being by taking a break/breath for a while (during informal practices), or for longer periods (during formal practices). We discover how we can change our mind patterns and our brains through mindfulness practices.

I am in our garden with my granddaughter. She is joyfully jumping around, stepping now and then on young spinach plants.

I say to her, "Hey, darling, let's help this spinach grow."

"How?"

"Just take a handful of soil, crumble it and then spread it around the plant." She takes the clod of soil and crumbles it in her hand. "Do you feel the soil crumbling in your hand?" I ask.

"Yeeeeaaah!" She smiles and puts the soil gently beside the plant before she continues to jump around with joy.

She may not remember this tiny mindful moment of feeling the soil in her hand, but she did experience it.

I continue to develop my own practice, along with ideas about how to teach people to nurture their minds by tuning in and acknowledging what's inside, before deciding how to respond wisely. This is a lifelong task. It is a gift to have such a task at the age of 66: one that I am grateful for. In my experience, there are no real cultural, age-related or religious boundaries for nurturing our minds – we all have the capacity to experience the benefits of mindfulness.

For me, mindfulness is a new literacy for healthier living: a new paradigm for living. In the same way that we might learn a language and move from understanding the basics to being able to read, write and think in this language, mindfulness can provide us with a new way of living: it becomes a part of how we work, love, cook . . . it becomes a part of every aspect of our lives.

Mindful Exercise:
A Mindful Break for a New Perspective

This exercise can help you to take a fresh perspective in any situation. It may be helpful when you are thinking about a challenging situation on your own, or even provide you with a mindful break to pause and reflect when you are caught up in a demanding situation while you are with someone.

1. Stop for a while. Sit or stand, eyes open or closed (whatever feels appropriate). Breathe in, breathe out.

2. Bring to mind what you think about the situation and/or the person involved – your judgements and opinions. Become aware of the thoughts and feelings that arise.

3. As best you can, step out of your thoughts about the situation or person. Become aware of your thoughts and feelings, and those the other person may be experiencing. Recognise that your boundless awareness contains it all. Really see the situation from this spacious perspective. Listen to the perspective of the other person. Feel their presence. Smile at them. Smile to yourself.

4. Become aware of how you feel when you step out of your thoughts and feelings about the situation or person – when you are simply smiling and being aware of both yourself and the situation or person. Try not to create a story around this new perspective: just be present.

5. Reflect on the situation from the perspective of yourself, the other person, and from a neutral third person. What difference does it make if you create this wide perspective from your spacious awareness?

After taking a mindful break like this, you may find it easier to reflect on your perspective with curiosity and an open mind, which might lead to wiser decisions and outcomes rather than a response driven by highly charged emotions.

Guided Meditation: Widening Perspective Meditation

Widening your perspective can help you to make wise, thoughtful decisions. This meditation guides you towards making a mental habit of widening your perspective. You may find the guidance helpful before you react or make a decision. You can listen to the audio at TeachMindfulnessOnline.com/transform.

About Magdalena Živković

Magdalena is a mindfulness teacher. She previously worked as a psychologist in the prison service, before retiring in 2009. She lives in Croatia and now teaches mindfulness in different settings.

http://www.zajednica.com.hr/en/

22

Mindfulness with Gammy:
Sharing Mindfulness with Your Family

~ Jane McGrade

Gazing out my windows, overlooking green grass and thick wooded forest – the cosy boundary of our backyard – I feel peaceful. I am enjoying watching deer grazing and ducks floating on the pond as if there isn't a care in the world. I gaze out the windows at the front of my home and I have the same feeling of peace. Here, in my little world, there is no evidence of the dangers of the coronavirus pandemic.

We are told to shelter at home, something I have never heard of before now. My children are working from home, my grandchildren are schooling at home, and my husband and I are far away from the rest of our family. When and how we will see them next, we have no idea.

To be worried about their health and wellbeing and to be separated does not sit well with me. In the past, I would have moped and sulked and been difficult to live with. Even though I knew there was nothing I could do about the situation, I would have wallowed in self-pity, sadness and worry. Thank goodness I don't choose to live that way anymore. I know what to do, so I will not spiral down that path.

I sit and I breathe. I sit and I breathe. I am practising mindfulness. As I sit, I am aware of my thoughts and feelings, but I continue to focus on my breath as I breathe in and out. My breathing slows, my body relaxes, and I feel calm. I do this for about fifteen minutes. I find that place of inner peace and acceptance and I know that I am okay. All is good. I smile and go on with my day.

We have always used FaceTime to connect regularly with our grandchildren, and we continued with that when the pandemic began to take hold. However, I started to notice that my grandchildren were often bored, unhappy and tired. Having to shelter at home is a difficulty they couldn't have anticipated, and they seemed lost as to how to handle it. They are teenagers, girls and boys aged 13–17, curious, intelligent, silly, edgy and critical. They are athletes, musicians, dancers and artists, who are used to living happy, active lives and hanging out with their friends.

What's the worst thing you can do to a teenager? Take away their social life and their freedom. The pandemic did just that. Deciding that action was required, I sent out a text to all the grandchildren to ask them to join me in a mindfulness practice every day at 5pm to help us all to connect in a positive way: Mindfulness with Gammy.

We begin our first meeting and I ask how they are doing. They all share that they are having difficulty falling asleep. Their routines have changed; in fact, there is little routine at all. They are confused and worried about what is happening and what will happen in future.

We begin talking about mindfulness: about why I practice, and how I believe practising mindfulness may be able to help them with their sleep. I give them one definition of mindfulness: paying attention, here and now, with kindness and curiosity – creating a space and an awareness of our thoughts and feelings so we can choose our response, our behaviour. We talk a little about it, and I am concerned that they are going to say, "Gammy, seriously, this is so boring! Pay attention to my breath? Are you kidding?" But no. They do not.

I am up front with them: "This may seem boring, but just humour me and try it out." So, we begin with a body scan. I am just seeing what happens, what our experience is. When we have finished with their first experience of practising a body scan, they say they feel relaxed and calm. They were surprised that they could feel sensations in their bodies as they were led from one area to the next. I couldn't have been happier or more surprised. Thank you, mindfulness!

We adjusted our schedules to practise mindfulness one day and yoga the next. We all liked getting together around 5pm because it was a transition for them from a day of studying to dinner time. They also said it was the only constant scheduled activity of the day, so they not only looked forward to our time together, but also they counted on it. In fact, one Sunday, when I thought we could perhaps take the day off, I received a text with a 'NO!!!' from my 13-year-old grandson. We met at 5pm that day.

Each time we meet for Mindfulness with Gammy, I give them a little more information about mindfulness and how it works to change your life. We have practised several different meditations and have had great discussions about gratitude and kindness and our thoughts and feelings. Learning mindfulness is like having a handbook with which to negotiate your life. You want to know what to do when you feel anxious or afraid of someone judging you? You want to know how to manage friendships? How to be your own best friend? What to do when you freeze taking a test or just before giving a speech?

Most of all, I want them to be happy being themselves. I want them to be their own best friend and spend time getting comfortable with who they are. We have explored happy thoughts and unpleasant ones and noticing in their bodies where they feel happiness and unhappiness. How to forgive yourself and others when a mistake has been made and then let it go. They loved the past, future and present meditation, and how they felt when they let go of the past and future. We talked about belief systems and expectations and negative self-talk, the teenage brain and trigger points. I am amazed at how much we have shared. They have been discovering their own safe space: the peaceful place that is inside all of us, the quiet voice that says, "I'm okay." The place where you discover gentle kindness and a caring, compassionate self. The place where you recognise non-judgement, true happiness and loving kindness.

It's been about two and a half months now of us meeting just about every other day for mindfulness. They keep showing up. They tell me they feel calmer and happier. They like how they feel, and they sleep well now.

Sharing mindfulness with my grandchildren has been an amazing experience, full of love and joy. The coronavirus pandemic has given us the space and time to be together enjoying being, just being. I am calmer and more confident about going forward and sharing mindfulness with other teens, so they too might find the benefits of mindfulness for themselves. May they know that loving kindness is their true nature and see the world from that perspective.

Mindful Exercise:
Mindful Listening

When someone is speaking to you, are you listening while checking your email or social media? Or looking away at something more interesting? Nowadays, multitasking is the norm: mindful listening, not so much.

Here is a mindful listening exercise you might like to try.

1. Choose a person you feel comfortable with and a fairly neutral subject to talk about. First, you will be the listener for three minutes and then you will be the person listened to for three minutes.

2. Turn off any devices and sit in a comfortable position, feeling the weight of your body on the chair. Notice what your feet feel like on the floor. Breathe in and out, noticing what your breath feels like in your belly. Relax your shoulders if you can and take another breath in and out.

3. Focus your attention on the speaker as they begin to talk. As you listen, can you tell if they are happy or not by their facial expression? Or by the tone of their voice? What is their body language like? Does this seem like an important topic to them? How does their voice sound? Are they moving their head, arms or hands while speaking? Are they engaging your attention?

4. Reverse the roles, taking your turn at being the speaker. You want to be heard. You want to be listened to. Connected with. You might notice cues from your listener that they are not tuned in to you. Or maybe they are focused on your every word. How can you tell? What is

your body language and what are you doing to engage your listener? Are you feeling listened to?

5. Reflect on how it felt to be both the speaker and the listener. You may want to share your observations with your partner after the exercise.

We know when we are not being listened to. We feel the disconnect and it hurts. But when we are present, listening and sharing with another person, we feel not only connected but valued, important, cared about and loved. Mindful listening is a simple but intimate act. An act of mind and heart.

Guided Meditation: Past, Future and Present Meditation

To be present – free of past baggage and future worries – is a gift of peace and joy. I invite you to try this guided meditation, which is one of our family favourites. You can hear the meditation at TeachMindfulnessOnline.com/transform.

About Jane McGrade

Jane has practised mindfulness and worked as a holistic educator for over 30 years. She was the director of holistic/complementary medicine at The National Empowerment Center, where she taught meditation and reiki. Mindfulness with Gammy is a four-week course for teens to bring mindfulness practices into their life.

www.one-mindful-breath.com

23

Mindful Parenting:
Becoming the Parent I Want to Be

~ Crysal Olds

Common wisdom is that once your baby is in your arms for the first time, you will feel joy unlike any other that you have ever felt in your life. Lying in the hospital bed, holding my beautiful little girl for the first time, I didn't feel this joy at all. I was grappling with fear; I felt wrenched from a world that I knew and was respected in and thrown into one drenched in uncertainty and 24/7 responsibility. I felt so alone. I hadn't read any parenting books while I was pregnant, as I was told I would instinctively know what to do. Well, I didn't. All I felt was a failure for not being prepared and, already, confirmation that I was a 'bad' mum. Where was this beautiful, accepting, joyful, respectful and compassionate parent I thought I would be? And what was holding me back from being the person I wanted to be, both for myself and for my child?

Through the first weeks of her life, my daughter was unable to sleep, except when she was lying on someone – which meant extreme sleep deprivation for me. After several days of just a couple of hours' sleep, I found myself on the couch, with her sleeping soundly on my chest. For some reason, in that moment, I let go of my thoughts and fears and focused on the weight of her on my chest, the difference in temperature between where she was and where she wasn't. I noticed the sound of her breathing, saw the relaxation and ease in her body as it moved with her breath. I noticed the sensation of my heart beating and my breath moving through my body, unaided, and free from restriction. I felt gratitude for the moment, and for my daughter. I felt acceptance of the sleeplessness and a sense of trust that she was doing what she needed to do – unaided and free from restriction, much like my breath. I found self-compassion, acceptance, and fulfilment in this moment and I felt detached from my inner critic: that little voice inside my head that would take any opportunity to reinforce the thought that I was a 'bad' mum. It was a breath of fresh air. I didn't know it then, but I was experiencing my first taste of mindfulness.

Throughout the coming months, this ability to let go of my thoughts and feelings, and to accept the moment for what it was and be present, came and went. I had snippets of this beautiful connection, but often my negative thoughts were stronger, overwhelming the observer inside me. I often struggled to find a way towards the feelings of joy, compassion, acceptance, impermanence and fulfilment that could connect us. I knew I had to find a way to make this feeling a part of my life on a regular basis.

I decided to research. I wanted to build a relationship with my child based on mutual respect, so I needed to find new ways of relating to her and myself. My rational mind also needed confirmation that what I intuited was best for my child was actually the 'right way' to parent her, because the information within me often conflicted with that of more seasoned parents.

I read many parenting books and when I found something that sang to me, I was like a kid with a new toy and I put it into action straight away. Some changes came easily to me, while others, even though I felt they were the way to go, were difficult – something kept holding me back. My thoughts and feelings fuelled me to react rather than respond in the heat of the moment, which was a major sticking point for me. When I started to investigate ways to manage my emotions, my thoughts and feelings, I found mindfulness.

I started researching different practices to bring more mindfulness into my life. Again, some things I picked up quickly, like using my breath as an anchor, being aware of my thoughts and feelings, and being curious. Naturally, however, some things took a bit more focus and discipline to cultivate on a regular basis – in particular, self-compassion and observing my thoughts and feelings without judgement or getting caught up in them, allowing them to simply be.

By this time, my daughter was nearly two years old, and I was struggling with being on 'toddler time'. I found being mindful helpful. For example, when I was asking her to hurry up, I would hear myself saying these words and be curious about them – Where did they come from? Why was I wanting to hurry her? – and the answers came.

When I was feeling bored waiting for my little girl to explore the world around her, I realised I had a choice: I could get curious and explore too – focusing on the sights, sounds, smells and textures around me – or I could push her along at my pace. During these moments, I noticed the gratitude and joy I felt for having experienced these moments of pure connection when I chose to be curious and play, as I let go of my attachments to how things 'should' be and instead focused on experiencing how events were unfolding.

When my daughter was angry or upset, I started to recognise that her behaviour was not naughty, but that she was asking for a need to be met. Letting go of any unrealistic expectations I had around her behaviour allowed me to connect with her in a compassionate, non-judgemental, respectful, kind and curious way. What's more, connecting in this way allowed her to be herself, free from defences.

I marvel at the immense power that self-compassion has over how I relate to myself and others. Where I am compassionate with myself, I can extend compassion to others. In areas of my life where self-compassion is a challenge for me (such as for parts of myself that I have yet to accept), I find it hard to be compassionate towards others in those areas too. Therefore everyone I meet – and especially my children on a daily basis – are a mirror, showing where I can accept myself and be compassionate towards myself, in order for me to live more fully as the parent and the person I want to be.

Discovering the kind of parent I wanted to be was as if I had stumbled upon the key to being available to coach my children through life respectfully, while also respecting myself. I felt a sense of freedom unlike any other – a sense that my future really was in my own hands. I was no longer held prisoner by my thoughts, feelings and intense emotions.

Of course, I am not perfect, and therefore neither is my mindfulness practice. Awareness is key to choosing our actions and behaviours, but sometimes we still choose ones that are not for our highest good. I still have periods of mindlessness, where I fall into autopilot and coast along those well-worn old paths, listening to my inner critic while I struggle to reconnect with myself and others. But awareness always returns – and once there is awareness, I can resume the mindful path with self-compassion, non-judgement and acceptance. I have learnt to accept responsibility and acknowledge any mindless behaviour, actions, gestures, or words said (or left unsaid), as well as repair any ruptures that these have led to.

In every moment that I have mindful awareness, I also have the choice – to choose the well-worn old path or the path where I am the parent and the person I want to be. Which do you choose?

Mindful Exercise:
Mindful Parenting

This short exercise helps you to choose your attitude before you engage with your child.

1. Before you engage with your child, take the time to be curious about yourself. What are you experiencing right now? What are your thoughts? What are your emotions? What bodily sensations are you experiencing? How is your breath – shortened and restricted, or full and free?

2. Look at your child – notice them as they are in that moment. Look at their facial expressions – what are they telling you? What sounds are they making? How are they holding their body? What movements are they making? What emotions might they be experiencing? Notice any reaction this has within you and breathe.

3. Be curious: what attitude might they need from you in this moment? Kindness? Curiosity? Compassion? Empathy? Non-judgement? Respect? Trust? Positive regard?

4. Repeat to yourself the attitude they need from you, and visualise yourself expressing that attitude.

5. Then, engage with your child.

This exercise may be helpful in times of transition or stress, maybe when everyone is trying to talk to you at the same time while you are getting dinner ready, or you're trying to get out of the house on time. Taking a step back to assess where you're at and what your children might need from you can take you out of an emotional response and into a more rational, higher-reasoning response.

Guided Meditation: The Parent You Want to Be

We all have an idea of the type of parent we want to be, the behaviours we want to exhibit and the attitudes we want to encourage in our children (and to live by ourselves). Yet, we all feel parental guilt when we fall short of our parenting ideal. In this visualisation, I invite you to go on a journey of self-discovery and uncover the nutrients you need to feed your parenting goal so you can show up as the parent you want to be. Listen to the audio track at <u>TeachMindfulnessOnline.com/transform</u>.

About Crysal Olds

Crysal lives in Nelson, New Zealand, and works with parents one-to-one and in group settings to help them step into being the parent they want to be. She has two children of her own.

www.mindovermatter.co.nz

24

Transforming Shame into Acceptance through Mindful Community

~ *Florence Scialom*

When I walked into my first group mindfulness session I felt nervous and unsure about what to expect, and what would be expected of me. As I sat down in a circle of about ten friendly strangers, someone handed me a cup of tea with a warm smile, and I began to relax. A sense of calm gratitude deepened in me as the session – and my experience with mindfulness – progressed. That day, I discovered that one of the most transformational aspects of practising mindfulness is the power of practising in a community.

It is a common misconception that the path of mindfulness leads directly to experiencing only calm and ease. In fact, the peace that practising mindfulness offers can unearth darker emotions and experiences that have previously been buried. Sadness, regret, anger . . . all can arise when practising mindfulness. This may sound intimidating, but recognising difficult emotions is a vital step towards healing.

My deeper emotions surfaced in the form of grief and shame. When I was 17, my mum took her own life after years of suffering from bipolar disorder. This was one of the darkest and most deeply painful experiences of my life, made even deeper and darker by the shame I carried about my mum's mental illness. As a teenage girl, I was often in denial about her suffering, and couldn't express the confusing emotions I had about my mum being unwell. When she died, I wanted to keep it as quiet as possible, reluctantly telling only a few of my closest friends.

This combination of grief and shame is something I've carried with me throughout my life, and I often experience it as a powerful prison, one that traps me inside myself in a way that makes me feel alienated, uncertain and inauthentic. I've often experienced the feeling that there is something deeply wrong with me, and that I cannot let my true self show for fear of being rejected.

Practising mindfulness and sharing in a group setting has allowed me to open up to my true feelings and experiences more than ever before. Where I feared rejection, I've been met with love and compassion. Where I feared isolation, I've been met with understanding and friendship. This has been a deeply healing balm to my inner anxieties, and it has made me feel more confident and loving towards myself and others.

Although my mind wandered wildly when I first started practising mindfulness with a group, I found a gentle sense of calm in allowing my thoughts to drift while all around me was still. I didn't try to stop my thoughts; being in a guided group gave me the time and motivation to simply observe them flowing through my mind. The more I learnt about mindfulness, the more I realised that this was actually part of the practice – not completely stopping my thoughts, but tuning into that observer in myself behind the constant chatter of my overactive mind.

During my first group session, I was also invited to take part in my first sharing circle. This involved deep, mindful listening and speaking from the heart, which was a revelation to me. I realised that it wasn't just me who had an overactive mind: all my niggling doubts, insecurities and fears were shared by others. Each person in the circle had their own story to tell, but each sharing held grains of universal truth from which everyone else could learn.

The transformation I experienced thanks to practising mindfulness in a community was made clear to me when my husband Thijs observed how much I'd opened up in recent years about the loss of my mum. Thijs and I have been together for over ten years, and he said that in the first six or seven years of our relationship I'd really struggle to talk about my mum at all, whereas now I am more able to openly share my experiences, emotions and reflections. This shift is not only the result of mindfulness – I have also needed therapy and other forms of support – but I know that the loving, mindful communities I have been held in have played a large part in my personal growth.

Another transformation I experienced is becoming a mum myself. My daughter Lilly was born on Mother's Day, 2019. I knew that becoming a parent would not be easy for me following my background with my own mum. But I did not realise just how difficult – and deeply transformative – it would be.

The sleep deprivation and not having my own mum around hit me very hard, and I began to experience symptoms of depression. I felt deeply sad, didn't take any joy in day-to-day events, and even contemplated taking my own life at times. The fleeting suicidal thoughts that crossed my mind acted as a red flag to get the help I so desperately needed. I was diagnosed with postpartum depression and began taking antidepressant medication and having therapy.

I realised I'd held a lot of judgement about my mum: the way I felt she had frequently abandoned me; the way her illness impacted her behaviour towards me and my siblings. After going through postpartum depression, I gained a deeper sense of compassion and understanding. The depression helped me to connect to my mum more, but also left me with a deep sense of pain at not being able to share with her: to take her hand, to talk with her, to try to understand together the deep uncertainties involved in motherhood. Yet, in her absence, she has taught me so much about the importance of asking for help, and about the value of finding spaces to be truly open with my most fragile inner experiences.

After receiving the help that I needed, the depression began to lift and I began to experience some joy in life again, and in parenting too. I began to connect more with my beautiful daughter, and to do the things that I love with her, including mindfulness meditation. Meditating looks a little different with a small baby around, but I began a regular morning sitting practice again, albeit in a shorter and more flexible way than before!

When Lilly was five months old, I took her on a mindfulness retreat. This went so well that I took her again when she was nine months old. On both occasions, what enabled me to be at the retreat with my baby daughter was the support from the wider community of retreat participants.

Mindfulness For Transformation

As the saying goes, it takes a village to raise a child. Thijs and I are very lucky to have active support from our families and some very sweet friends, too. I have been so grateful to find that my 'village' also includes the wider community of people I know through practising mindfulness.

Practising mindfulness with a community offers opportunities for ongoing transformation, enabling a loving acceptance through life's ups and downs. It has helped me to deal with dark experiences and emotions, as well as providing me with support and kindness while raising my daughter. My mindfulness practice is ongoing, as are my experiences of being in mindful communities and on my own personal development journey.

The next stage of my journey is to move further into teaching and facilitating mindfulness in groups, and I've found this to be a role I really love. A sense of community looks different for everyone, but community has the potential to be good for everyone, too.

Messages from wider society can encourage us to live our lives as if we can make it alone, but at some point we receive a wake-up call to show us how beautiful it is to need each other.

Mindful Exercise:
Mindful Listening and Speaking

This exercise will help you practise your skills of deep listening and speaking from the heart, which are both vital for building mindfulness in community.

1. Find someone who you would be happy to do a deep mindful listening exercise with for 15–20 minutes. Each person has three turns to speak for two minutes, and three turns to listen, with a period of sharing together at the end.

2. Use a phone or timer to time each turn.

3. Sit across from each other, and take a short time just to get comfortable and arrive together in your shared space, maybe by taking a minute of shared silence and/or a few deep, grounding breaths together.

4. Choose who will speak first. The person speaking is invited to share openly from the heart answers to the following question: *Which feelings, emotions and experiences are most present in your life right now?* The person listening is invited to listen mindfully without responding. (The person listening first needs to set a timer for two minutes and gently let the person know when it is time to switch; speaker becoming listener, and listener becoming speaker.)

5. Repeat this process three times.

6. After you have both spoken and listened three times, set aside a slightly longer period (for example, 5–10 minutes) to simply reflect together on your experience. What arose for you in having this time to share and being deeply

listened to? What was it like to try to mindfully stay present while listening to the other?

The point of this exercise is not to respond to or comment on what is shared, but rather to practise mindful presence with another person.

Guided Meditation: Mindful Community and Self-compassion Practice

This guided mindfulness meditation is inspired by self-compassion practices and based on the work of the researcher Kristin Neff, amongst others.

This practice guides you to be mindful of what is present right now, in your body, and your feelings and thoughts; to accept that there is a commonality in all human experiences and to respond to yourself with kindness. Listen to the guided meditation at TeachMindfulnessOnline.com/transform.

About Florence Scialom

Florence is a trained facilitator and mindfulness teacher. She is the Communications Manager at the Network of Wellbeing (NOW). Originally from the UK, Flo lives in Rotterdam in the Netherlands with her husband Thijs and her daughter Lilly.

https://mindfulchangeblog.wordpress.com

25

Compassion in Action: Understanding Others and Remembering to Be Kind

~ *Julie Hayes*

I came out of the prison hall really happy with the mindfulness session I'd just run, feeling grateful for the feedback from the offenders. As I queued to hand my keys back to security, I heard a voice say, "Hello Julie." My heart sank into the depths of my stomach: it was Katie, the manager of a charity I had once worked for.

The last time I had seen her, I was informed that my services were no longer required: with no notice, I was asked to clear my desk and leave. I was left high and dry without a job and with a mortgage to pay. I remember that day so vividly. There had been a euphoric moment of recognising that I was standing utterly on my own and had to be as strong and as authentic as I had ever been in my life. The question of "How do I pay my bills?" mixed with the excitement of what was next for me – a truly mindful moment, indeed!

So, here I was running mindfulness courses in prisons: happy, content and doing a job I loved, one where I was valued. Yet just hearing Katie's voice raised emotions that were just as strong as if the redundancy had happened yesterday. Somehow, I focused on my breathing and responded to her politely.

A couple of weeks later, I received an email from head office to inform me that I would be taking the lead on a collaborative project with another organisation. I was excited about the opportunity, until I read the name of the organisation and realised who I would be working alongside.

You guessed it: Katie.

I consider myself an insightful person; a passionate mindfulness teacher who has always been focused on active acceptance of what is. When loss and hurt make appearances in my life, I try to take the opportunity to ask myself, "What is this teaching me?", "Where is my growth?" and "How is this serving me?" But, somehow, it felt harder to ask these questions this time.

I couldn't help but replay events from the past. The pull was too strong to ignore. I knew I had to navigate myself through this situation carefully and gently. So I made a list of all the benefits and insights that I had gained since redundancy, which reminded me of how I had grown. I reflected on my strengths and wondered, if I hadn't lost that job, would it be fair to say that I might not be in the place I was now? However, I still felt defensive and slightly intimidated. I wasn't floating about, feeling all Zen and connected to everybody and everything. When I began creating a scenario in my head about our first meeting and how I felt it would go, I felt anxiety well up inside me.

The day arrived for our first meeting together. The universe did give me a gentle hug by allowing the meeting to be held on familiar ground: in my office. That morning I did a kindness meditation to help me prepare, and on the way into work I reminded myself that I am an observer: this meant that, yes, there was a feeling of nervousness, but I wasn't the anxiety, and the feeling would pass. Being an observer reminded me to take a step back.

I arrived early and prepared the room, opened the window and rearranged my crystals. I did some deep breathing and allowed my emotions and feelings to rise and fall without putting any expectation on myself for things to be any other way. The director of the company arrived first, and we exchanged polite chit-chat. She asked me if I was okay with the situation. At that point I felt my defences rising, but I redirected myself to use my breath as an anchor so that I could respond calmly and confirm that it wasn't a problem. Maybe I wasn't being totally truthful, but I am not perfect; just a human being trying to be my best self.

Katie arrived, and what I noticed immediately was her lack of eye contact. In that moment, my heart softened towards her and some of my defensiveness faded away. We began the meeting, and I was able to observe our interactions. Katie had always come across as wanting to be 'the planner', the one in control, and she was expressing those same patterns again.

I remembered how my fellow colleagues from my old job would say that Katie worked long hours and weekends, very rarely smiled, never delegated and kept a tight control of the staff under her management. For somebody like me who needs a certain amount of room to be creative, I had found her approach suffocating. It now dawned on me that she was a perfectionist, and what a difficult burden that must be for her. We agreed on some actions to carry forward and scheduled a meeting for four weeks later.

At the next meeting, Katie produced the action plan we had mutually devised, but she presented it in such a way that it looked like the majority of the ideas were hers. I wanted to challenge her, but I had an insight in that moment that she needed the credit and recognition more than I did. All of a sudden I saw beyond the words; I felt them, and something happened inside me – I let go. It felt like compassion in action, and as if a weight had been lifted from my shoulders.

This was a turning point in our relationship. I'm not saying we became the best of friends, but we became better friends than we had ever been before. The project was a success and was rolled out to three further prisons. Today, as I write this, I am thankful for the gift that is mindfulness. In that particular scenario, mindfulness helped my resistance fall away and allowed me to find compassion for another human being when they needed it.

I may not sit on a fluffy carpet, all Zen, but my passion for mindfulness is contagious. If you see a middle-aged woman walking around with a sandwich board around her neck, espousing the benefits of mindfulness, you guessed it – it's me!

Mindfulness has taught me to let go a little, to trust more and not to be so attached to outcomes. It allows me to be lighter, gentler and kinder to myself. I often wonder if Katie ever experiences the lighter side of life and feels able to be kind to herself, but at least I now understand her need for control and why she is the way she is. It is simply part of her journey.

I would like to share an affirmation I use daily – if it resonates, please use it too!

I am grateful for the opportunities that allow kindness and compassion to flow from me and to me. I always feel rested, refuelled and revived.

Mindful Exercise:
Compassionate Resilience

Empathy is one of the greatest gifts you can share with another human being or animal. However, being constantly empathic can leave you feeling depleted and running on empty. Many ancient teachings espouse the importance of compassion and kindness to yourself. In the following exercise, I invite you to declutter and re-energise your internal world, spending a few moments practising self-compassion.

1. Draw three large balloons.

2. In the first balloon, write three beliefs you feel hold you back and no longer serve you. For example, "Everything has to be perfect for me to be happy" or "I need others' approval to feel okay". (Remember that a belief is nothing more than a long-held thought.)

3. Place your hands on your heart. If it feels okay to do so, visualise releasing the balloon along with the beliefs inside it.

4. Write three positive words your friends and family often use to describe you in the second balloon. For example, 'dependable' or 'generous'. With your hands on your heart, take a moment to breathe in those warm, heartfelt words, lodging them deep in your heart as a reminder for when life feels tough. Visualise tying the balloon to your right hand.

5. Reflect on three self-care routines that replenish and revitalise you, such as getting a massage or meeting a friend for coffee. Write them in the third balloon as a

gentle reminder to make time for them. Visualise tying this balloon to your left hand.

You have released one balloon, and you have two more balloons, one either side of you, to keep you afloat, filled with gentle reminders of kindness and self-compassion.

Guided Meditation: Self-compassion Meditation

This guided meditation brings focus and awareness to your heart space, allowing you to gently cultivate self-compassion. I invite you to accept for yourself the loving words and thoughts you offer so readily to others. Listen to the meditation at TeachMindfulnessOnline.com/transform.

About Julie Hayes

Julie has been a holistic teacher, mindfulness practitioner and transformational life coach for over a decade, helping people to help themselves. Mindfulness has taken her on an amazing journey, and she believes that every day presents something new.

www.juliehayesholisticwellness.co.uk

26

Channelling My Creativity into Mindful Sketching

~ *Rebecca O'Connor*

I discovered meditation following a hysterectomy aged 36. I was at my lowest point ever – coming to terms with the fact that I wouldn't have children was crushing, and I didn't know how I'd ever get back to being myself.

Poor health has never been far away: it's what led me to having a hysterectomy in the first place. It has influenced and controlled my life in a number of ways over the years – from my earliest memories of being a sickly child, to discovering that my allergies brought on asthma attacks. I was eventually diagnosed with an autoimmune disease.

The mental health implications of living with what is often an invisible illness take their toll, affecting me every day. Some days are better than others, but I have no way of knowing when my next flare-up will occur.

After my hysterectomy, I was in a very dark place: exhausted and in constant pain that kept me awake most nights. My doctor referred me for counselling, and I was later introduced to meditation and cognitive behavioural therapy (CBT), but I still felt as though something was missing.

I was introduced to mindfulness meditation about two years ago, while I was recuperating from what should have been routine surgery (which unfortunately took a dramatic turn, resulting in permanent, debilitating pain). I attended a lovely group class, and I made steady progress. The breathing anchor meditation, body scan and compassionate acceptance all helped me massively – I felt that I really connected with myself and my surroundings. My mum was even inspired to take up mindfulness (or, as she calls it, 'tummy breathing'), and she attends a weekly class at her local library aged 81!

Trying to fit in classes around a demanding job, my busy home life and regular periods of ill-health wasn't easy, so I decided to download a mindfulness app to keep to a regular practice. However, I couldn't ignore my deafening and overwhelming negative self-talk, which told me that I had to 'prove' that my health wasn't going to hold me back. This negative desire to prove myself, combined with the long hours at work, led to me living on a hamster wheel of stress, exhaustion and, ultimately, burnout. I didn't make it easy for myself either – if I felt I was having a good day, I'd subconsciously decide to push myself harder than ever, before inevitably crashing and not being able to get out of bed for days at a time. (I later learnt that this is called 'pacing' – easy to say, not easy to practise if you're driven and ambitious!) I knew something had to change if I was going to be able to manage my health and emotional wellbeing in an effective and helpful way.

I felt as if I had already reinvented myself so many times in response to my health and other factors beyond my control, so committing to changing my behaviour was tough. Writing encouraging notes and mantras to myself and popping them in my notebook, as well as mindful sketching and other creative pursuits, really helped me stay on track, even when I felt lousy or just couldn't calm the voices in my head. Sometimes my brain felt over-stimulated and I struggled to calm it sufficiently to meditate, but when this happened I would give myself permission to simply sit and focus on my breath to help me feel more rested, which was hugely beneficial for my constant fatigue.

My practice developed further. I realised that by combining mindful creativity and sketching, my overall experience of mindfulness became deeper and more profound every time, especially if I was experiencing mindfulness in nature: in the countryside, local park or beside the sea. Doing something creative effortlessly draws you in to the present moment and invites curiosity, no 'talent' or previous training required. (Later, I would discover the term 'biophilia': the hypothesis that human beings possess an innate emotional affiliation to nature. In my mind, this explained why my mindful sketching walks in nature had such a powerful effect!)

When my sight deteriorated and I had to stop driving (which coincided with the coronavirus pandemic lockdown in March 2020), I was suddenly limited to my garden. I began to pay attention to all the plants and flowers, and the comings and goings of its visitors (those with feathers, spines or fur). Mindful creativity helped me to continue to incorporate mindfulness into my daily life: that feeling of literally 'coming to my senses', whether it's through observing shapes, colours, textures, sounds, or the scent or taste of something.

The desire to create is powerful. It fuels our desire to be curious, experimental and adventurous. When years of ill health left me feeling exhausted and suffering with burnout, mindful creativity provided me with a way towards a happier, healthier and more peaceful life. I feel as if I have discovered my very own superpower – by combining mindfulness with sketching and painting, and even baking, I find I am always making and creating!

By accepting the process itself with kindness and embracing this immersive state of flow, I have been able to focus on being creative and developing a flexible sense of self. I feel empowered that I'm managing to get through the coronavirus pandemic restrictions with a growth mindset, focusing on learning and growing. I've signed up to another course, made more social connections, and I'm enjoying collaborating with another mindfulness coach as part of developing my mindfulness training. I understand myself much better: I'm feeling invigorated, my mood is lighter and I feel optimistic. Mindful creativity, particularly mindful sketching, is an essential part of my daily routine.

I continue to be a work in progress, but since discovering meditation and mindfulness, I'm more self-aware: I get on with life, make adjustments here and there, and embrace the importance of self-care. Above all, I adopt a mindful and creative approach to my long-term wellbeing.

For me, mindful creativity has evolved into a powerful combination of focusing on my breath, using it as an anchor, and making that deep connection with the world around me – it's like seeing something really clearly for the very first time. By focusing on the present moment, we have a perfect opportunity to explore and develop healthy habits, introducing things that nurture our wellbeing and enable us to flourish as individuals.

Mindful Exercise:
Creativity for Wellbeing – Draw Your Breath, Calm Your Mind

This mindful sketching exercise will help you regain a sense of presence. You can practice mindful sketching at any time – perhaps in the garden or park, in a café, at work or at home (in fact, anywhere when you find yourself feeling 'stuck' or overwhelmed). You don't need any 'talent' or previous experience of drawing to do the exercise.

You will need a sheet of paper and a pencil (or pen, if you prefer).

1. Look at your piece of paper: what colour do you see? Is it bright-white or off-white, the same colour all over, or is some of it in shade? Half close your eyes and soften your gaze: is there anything else to observe, any patterns, letters or numbers?

2. Fold the paper in half, rubbing your finger along the fold.

3. Place your pencil between your thumb and first two fingers. Close your eyes and notice the shape and texture of the pencil. Is it smooth or angular? Feel the sensation of the pencil between your fingers and thumb.

4. Roll the pencil between your fingers and thumb. Take a deep breath in through your nose, and slowly exhale as you feel the weight of the pencil and the balance shifting as you roll it. Continue to feel your breath. As you inhale deeply, feel your ribs expand; as you let go, feel your shoulders relax and any tension soften.

5. Place the point of the pencil anywhere on the paper, leaning against a hard surface (such as a table) if possible.

Taking a long, slow breath, look around to identify something to draw, perhaps an object that you have only just noticed. Take a deep breath and allow your pencil to 'wander', making a sketch of the object. The idea is to make marks and be playful, not to replicate the object precisely. Observe the object: the edges, the spaces and the relationships between them; the light and shadow around the object, before finally considering it as a whole. Alternate the pressure on the pencil to represent light and shade, while continuing to focus on your breath.

6. After several minutes of mark-making, turn over the piece of paper. Take a few deep, meaningful breaths, and reflect – what thoughts come to mind? You may wish to note them down on the blank side of the piece of paper.

Repeat this exercise when you find yourself needing to focus or re-energise yourself.

Guided Meditation: Mindful Sketching

By bringing an attitude of playfulness and curiosity to this mindful sketching meditation, you can develop a willingness to open up your senses and achieve a richer awareness as you nurture a sense of compassion towards yourself. It's all about being present in the moment as you create something. Listen to the guided meditation at TeachMindfulnessOnline.com/transform.

About Rebecca O'Connor

Rebecca lives in the beautiful North East of England. She is a trained creative artist, qualified life coach and accredited mindfulness teacher. She lives with her husband and their two Maine Coon cats, Starbo and Zimmie. She has developed a platform to help others on their own creative journey with mindfulness.

www.mindfulsketcher.com

27

Connecting with Nature to Find My Inner Compass

~ Clare Snowdon

I had spent much of my life struggling with difficult feelings and emotions. I was constantly trying to fix myself, and I was heavily self-critical. The underlying message from these struggles led me to believe that I wasn't good enough.

Gradually, with medication and changes in my life circumstances, I was able to get back to a healthier state. I still used food and retail 'therapy' to deal with difficult experiences, but I was more concerned about the resulting sense of being cut off from many of my feelings and memories. I really struggled to get in touch with what I was thinking or feeling so that I could deal with it, which made any kind of therapy very tricky.

In 2013, a member of a group I was part of talked about meditation. I was intrigued, so I started using an app on my smartphone. I just followed the course of the guided meditations, but I wasn't entirely sure what I was doing it for. Still, I kept coming back to it.

In these early stages of practising meditation, I thought that I was supposed to be free of my thoughts, which clearly was not the case. I believed that I was trying to achieve a particular state of mind and that it was possible to do it perfectly if I just did all the right things! I kept persevering, though.

As my practice continued, I started to notice being much more conscious in everyday life away from the formal practices. I had tried other informal practices – mindful toothbrushing and so on – but I was beginning to experience moments of being mindful without having a specific intention to be present. This shift in my behaviour meant that I could catch myself before I reacted thoughtlessly or made a choice I would later regret. It enabled me to make wiser choices.

I was starting to build a relationship with my feelings, rather than trying to avoid them or smother them. I approached my thoughts like a scientist, with curiosity, noticing patterns of thinking but not trying to fix them or replace them. I saw the choices I had more clearly, and I used the phrase 'thoughts are not facts' as a kind of mantra to invite the possibility that I might be interpreting my experience in a way that was not necessarily true or helpful. In particular, I was able to sit with acutely anxious feelings and just get curious about what it was like to feel anxious. I would ask myself, "Am I okay in this moment?" Invariably, the answer was "Yes!"

Anxiety is often about what might happen or involve a sense that something could go wrong. Before, I had been using a lot of energy and losing sleep due to worrying. Meditation was no longer just about sitting and hitting the pause button on a stressful day: it was starting to open the door to a new way of living and experiencing life.

This was so transformational that I felt I wanted to share it with others. I decided to train as a mindfulness teacher with Shamash Alidina, where I was introduced to the idea of kindfulness. I understood that compassion was a key ingredient of mindfulness, but hearing about this new perspective – using kindness, warmth and friendliness in my mindfulness practice – helped me to start including myself and my feelings in that compassionate bubble.

My biggest reservation after completing my training to teach mindfulness was that I wasn't qualified as a therapist. I was most mindful in natural environments and knew that this was something I wanted to share, but I had yet to find my voice. My limiting belief of not being good enough resurfaced.

To counter this belief, I trained as a mental health first aider and as a mindfulness champion at work, where I helped to run mindfulness taster sessions. I learnt to share my experiences in such groups.

Later, an amazing opportunity arose for me to train to be a natural mindfulness guide with Ian Banyard. I was finding my voice through connecting with nature and sharing that experience with others. It really helped me to get out of my comfort zone and step forward. The real breakthrough for me was feeling safe and supported in nature. This allowed me to truly listen to the deep wisdom that I found beyond my conditioned way of being in the world – I could be myself, I felt at home, and I could trust my experience.

I love encouraging others to share my experiences in nature – it could be as simple as connecting with the senses (hearing rustling leaves, for example) or discovering an insight or lesson (such as watching how deer quickly return to grazing after a fright – they are a great example of living in the moment!).

Tuning in to the clues and signs in nature can also be rewarding, such as knowing when and where I can expect to see bats. Mindfulness is key here – becoming aware of signs that are often hard to articulate, perhaps as a combination of weather and light conditions. I am passionate about helping people to discover how they can benefit from a better connection with nature – there is nothing quite like seeing the awe and wonder in someone else's face! – and how they, in turn, can look after the natural environment.

There is an additional ingredient, a spiritual element, in my mindfulness journey that's important to note: my inner compass. This means different things to different people. I believe that we have an inherent sense of purpose – some might call this knowing right from wrong – and interconnectedness. Mindfulness gives me an awareness of when I am aligned with that inner compass. It is possible to move towards this intellectually, with an intention to cultivate qualities such as compassion and kindfulness. However, with practice, I have come to recognise the signals within myself that tell me when I am wandering off course – even in the middle of a conversation. I don't need to know the exact origin or nature of this inner compass; I don't believe there's anything mystical about it. It is there for people to discover for themselves if they want to. I have come to realise that my inner compass points me towards a life aligned with my values and that this is a very powerful way to live.

My experience has shown me that in sharing our own stories, we can help other people with theirs. The single biggest thing I ever did for my mental health was to ask for help. How can we do that if we feel unable to talk about our stories; if we feel as if they are something to be afraid of?

Mindfulness has helped me to stop avoiding life and hiding behind my fears. It has helped me to see that anxiety can be a strength. I stay alert for my inner compass guiding me towards actions to help myself or others. Above all, I have learnt to embrace and express my authentic self: I have realised that I am okay just as I am. It is my great hope that others will follow a similar journey and find, as I have, that our challenges can unlock a really rich and purposeful existence that is just waiting to be discovered.

Mindful Exercise:
The Spacious Bubble

Among so many other things, mindfulness has taught me to be playful and to stop taking everything so seriously! Here's a short, playful exercise that you can try (either with a soap bubble mixture or simply by visualising a bubble) to encourage a mindful response to minor challenges.

1. Take a small challenging thought or emotion and visualise blowing it into a bubble (whether real or imagined).

2. Observe the bubble mindfully. Pay attention to the qualities of the bubble itself; the colours and texture. Become aware of other feelings apart from the challenging one – maybe even a sense of gentle playfulness. You are not trying to make the thoughts or feelings go away; instead, you are seeing if it is possible to hold these thoughts or feelings more gently in your awareness. These thoughts and feelings exist alongside other parts of your experience – they're not the only thing.

3. Invite other, less challenging things into your sphere of awareness, such as noticing the blue sky as well as the clouds. You have created a little space around the thought or emotion, which allows for a more mindful response.

When a challenging thought or emotion is present, it can consume our entire focus. There is no space around it to see past it or through it. However, instead of thinking, "I am anxious," try noting that "There is anxiety here." It's not 'my' anxiety and doesn't define me as a person, it's just part of my experience in that moment.

Guided Meditation: Weather Station

Many years ago, I worked on a farm and was absolutely amazed by the lady I worked for, who would say, "It's going to rain in 45 minutes," and invariably she would be right. At the time it seemed like magic! However, I now realise that most of us have become so out of touch with the clues and signs from our own senses and their relation to the world around us that we have lost this ability. So here is a short meditation that you can have fun with, rediscovering your own forgotten superpowers! It takes a little practice, but I have come to tune in to when it will be 'flying ant day' or when I might see bats flying over my garden. You can listen to the meditation at TeachMindfulnessOnline.com/transform.

About Clare Snowdon

Clare is a mindfulness teacher and mindful nature connection guide, guiding others to use mindfulness to connect deeply with themselves, with others and with the world around them in a way that encourages compassion and a desire to care for the natural world.

www.dragonmindfulness.co.uk

Appendix:
Audio Tracks

To listen to the free guided meditations that come with this book, visit: TeachMindfulnessOnline.com/transform.

Introduction: Finding Meaning through Mindfulness and the Observer Self by Shamash Alidina – *Mindfulness of Senses*

Part I: Finding the Courage to Manage Challenging Experiences

Chapter 1: Finding Peace and Mutual Acceptance in the Present Moment by Nicky Minter – *Peace and Kindness Meditation*

Chapter 2: Transcending Chronic Depression by Fennel Waters – *Finding Your Way Back to Yourself* *

Chapter 3: Making Friends with Anxiety by Robyn Zagoren – *Mindful and Kindful Body Scan*

Chapter 4: Overcoming Performance Anxiety by Wendy Malko – *Public Speaking Visualisation*

Chapter 5: Overcoming Anxiety and Encouraging Creativity by Sarah Spiers – *Wake Up Fresh*

Chapter 6: Finding Understanding and Acceptance by Jennifer Gilroy – *Peaceful Freedom in Nature*

Chapter 26: Channelling My Creativity into Mindful Sketching by Rebecca O'Connor – *Mindful Sketching*

Chapter 27: Connecting with Nature to Find My Inner Compass by Clare Snowdon – *Weather Station*

*Guided Meditation Music Credits: 'The Transience Of Everything' by Ave Air. Via www.epidemicsound.com/

Printed in Great Britain
by Amazon